D1231466

Hutterites

The Nine

Our Story to Freedom

> About the cover

"But unto you that fear My name shall the Sun of righteousness arise with healing in His wings;…"
(Malachi 4:2)

Jesus is compared to the sun's rising and through His beams of light He offers deliverance, restoration, health, and refreshing.

Published by:
Risen Son Publishing

[1] Excerpts reprinted from *Peter Riedemann's Hutterite Confession of Faith*, translated and edited by John J. Friesen. Copyright © 1999 by Herald Press, Waterloo, Ont. Published simultaneously in the U.S. by Herald Press, Scottdale, PA. All rights reserved. Used by permission.

Unless otherwise indicated all Scripture quotations are taken from the King James Version of the Bible.

ISBN: 978-0-9895184-0-6
Library of Congress Control Number: 2013912186

Published by:
Risen Son Publishing

Please visit our website:
www.thenine9.com
Online ordering is available

Printed in Canada

This complete work is dedicated to our Lord and Savior Jesus Christ...

We, the nine, are presenting this work with the love of God in truth without any bitterness, unforgiveness or resentment towards the Hutterites or any other human being, race, color, or creed. We are witnesses with personal experiences founded upon factual truths and close observations.

Our hearts' motive, without reservation, is to proclaim boldly the Word of God as it is written, that people may find salvation, healing, and freedom in the Lord, Jesus Christ.

It is a blessing to serve God by keeping his commands to love God, love others, and preach the Word as Jesus commanded.

"Preaching the kingdom of God, and teaching those things which concern the Lord Jesus Christ, with all confidence, no man forbidding him." (Acts 28:31)

[1] "The Spirit of the Lord GOD is upon me; because the LORD hath anointed me to preach good tidings unto the meek; he hath sent me to bind up the brokenhearted, to proclaim liberty to the captives, and the opening of the prison to them that are bound;"

[2] "To proclaim the acceptable year of the LORD, and the day of vengeance of our God; to comfort all that mourn;"

[3] "To appoint unto them that mourn in Zion, to give unto them beauty for ashes, the oil of joy for mourning, the garment of praise for the spirit of heaviness; that they might be called trees of righteousness, the planting of the LORD, that he might be glorified." (Isa. 61:1-3)

3

As you read through these pages, the words being expressed may well challenge your perspective regarding Christianity.

It is our hope that your eyes will confirm the truth to your heart.

There is a time in the life of all created human beings when they come to a place of decision as to what they will determine as truth. This is an opportunity to question what you believe and why.

This is the story of nine courageous people who escaped the rigors of religiosity within a system in which they were born and raised. Choosing life outside of the colony cost them the future of family ties and the places they once called home. They were soon confronted with unimaginable obstacles as they were thrust into the "English world." To heal and overcome the emotional hurts and scars that were visited upon them, the distorted mindsets, behaviors, and habits had to be renounced and abandoned. They began to learn a graceful balance in life, expressing love and joy rather than extremes of anger and rage.

The nine were mostly unaccustomed to practical, everyday activities and essential skills in the "English world." Each of them had to be taught how to clearly and effectively communicate, to relate and express his or her heart socially. The very basics had to be taught, including clothing, proper hygiene, and etiquette. Having learned to be resourceful and personally responsible, they now operate and prevail in various successful businesses.

How these nine came to make their decision to leave all and find a new life is written in each of their own personal chapters.

Sincerely,
Those that received them

ACKNOWLEDGMENTS

To those Hutterites, ex-Hutterites, and those outside colony life, who have inspired us to write this book: Thank you for your prayers, support, and encouragement to fulfill this vision.

Throughout the process of writing this book we have received much welcome counsel and direction in editing, publishing, and printing to complete this work for God's glory.

Again, thank you for helping to spread the gospel of Jesus Christ and bring hope to those longing for The Truth.

TABLE OF CONTENTS

FOREWORD

Is this the time when God has said, "Enough"?

Yes! He has seen the affliction of His people.

"And the LORD said, <u>I have surely seen</u> the affliction of my people which are in Egypt, and have heard their cry by reason of their taskmasters; for I know their sorrows;" (Ex. 3:7)

The Egyptians were oppressing God's people in Egypt. God promised to set them free from slavery. God used His miraculous power to lead them out of Egypt into a good land flowing with milk and honey.

God kept His promise and used a man by the name of Moses to lead His people out of Egypt. If Moses had not stood in the breach for them, God's people would have been destroyed.

"Therefore he said that he would destroy them, had not Moses his chosen stood before him in the breach, to turn away his wrath, lest he should destroy them." (Psa. 106:23)

We are standing in the gap for those who find themselves in a similar situation; by showing the way out so they can persevere and overcome. We know and understand that God has a strategy to write our testimonies and the outcome is entirely in His hands.

We are humbled and recognize the privileged responsibility we have been given in writing this book.

If you, the reader, find yourself in an oppressive situation, seek the Lord Jesus Christ with a sincere heart for He is faithful to His Word. With Jesus Christ there is no limit to what He will do for you. He will move all of heaven and earth to move you to where He wants you to be. It is a place of freedom and liberty.

Our prayer is that you will experience the will of God for your life, in power and in truth.

To God be all the glory for who He is…

and for all His wonders!

Who are the Hutterites?

There are about 45,000 Hutterites living in colonies with approximately 100 people per colony. The colonies are located in middle and western Canada, and upper Midwest and northwest United States. Hutterites originated during the Reformation in the 1500s when many people were breaking away from the Roman Catholic Church. Some who broke away found that infant baptism was not according to the Word of God and were rebaptized as adults, beginning the Anabaptist movement. The Amish, Mennonites, and Hutterites all came from the Anabaptist movement and consider themselves spiritual cousins. Hutterites are similar to the Amish and Mennonites in doctrine and dress but differ in their communal way of life. Hutterites are separated into three groups: the Lehrerleut, Dariusleut, and the Schmiedeleut. These differ slightly in customs and dress but agree in doctrine and day-to-day life. Hutterites all speak a German dialect unique only to themselves.

Hutterite colonies are rural and most of their income is agriculturally based with manufacturing becoming more common. Hutterites do most of their own labor: constructing buildings, maintenance and repair on equipment, making clothes, butchering and growing food, etc.

Hutterite colonies are male-managed with women participating in traditional roles such as cooking, housekeeping, gardening, and sewing. Women have no formal vote in the decision-making power in a colony.

Hutterites have a strictly regulated dress code. Traditionally, men wear black pants, suspenders and a homemade buttoned shirt, and women wear a homemade dress and black head covering. Married men are required to wear a beard.

Each colony has three or four high-level leaders to include one or two ministers, the secretary, and the farm boss. The minister or ministers are the spiritual leaders and regulate the daily life of the members in the colony. The secretary is in charge of the finances. The farm boss is in charge of farming operations.

Everything is owned by the colony and all individual efforts are for the furthering of the colony. All earnings go to one or more bank accounts, which are controlled and accessed only by the leaders. Individuals are paid an allowance of $3.00 to $5.00 dollars per month. Basic necessities are provided for by the colony: food, clothing, and shelter. In turn, it is demanded that one's life be fully devoted to the Hutterian way of life.

Hutterite life is very structured and ruled by tradition. Daily church services are conducted in High German. Men sit on one side and women on the other, in order from oldest to youngest. This is mandatory from age five onward.

Three meals a day are held in the communal dining hall. Again, men sit on one side of the dining hall with women on the other, according to age. Children eat in a separate dining hall until they turn 15 years of age. Turning 15 is a monumental experience because one is then considered an adult, entering the adult work force.

At age 2½ Hutterite children start attending Kindergarten, where they are taught by the elder women. Formal education begins at age five when Hutterite children attend both "English" and German school. German school lasts two hours each day. A German teacher is selected from the male married members of the colony to teach the Hutterite religion and the German language. English schooling consists of public curriculum but is still located on colony premises. The English teacher has to be accredited according to government standards. In most cases this is a non-Hutterite since most Hutterites are not permitted to attend college. Generally speaking, English education fulfills the basic government standards so a person can continue the daily Hutterite life.

Most of the colonies are arranged in a similar fashion. The communal kitchen and church are centrally located with living quarters adjacent. Schools, butchering plant, and shops are built fairly close to the houses, while barns and garden are located on the outskirts.

Here is a layout of what a typical Hutterite colony might look like.

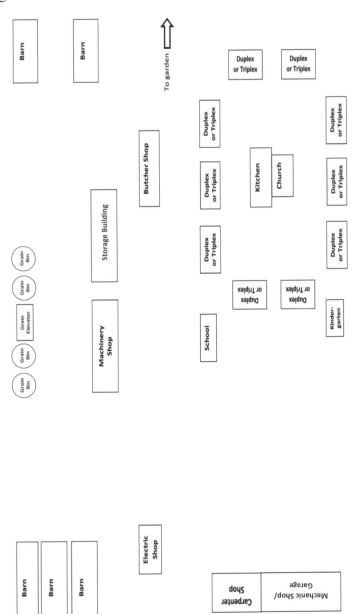

CHAPTER 1

The Foundation Of Hutterite Life

Jacob Hutter was the Anabaptist leader most influential in shaping the group that became known as Hutterites.

Peter Riedemann is considered the second founder because of his writings explaining the Hutterite faith. Peter Riedemann was born in 1506 in what is now Poland. When in prison for his faith in the early 1540s Peter Riedemann wrote the Confession of Faith for the Lutheran ruler Phillip of Hesse, to sum up the Hutterite-Anabaptist beliefs and way of life. This confession is approved by the Hutterites as the definitive statement of their faith.

The Hutterites separate themselves from the rest of society with an outward appearance of holiness, claiming to be true followers of Jesus Christ.

"And Jesus knew their thoughts, and said unto them, Every kingdom divided against itself is brought to desolation; and every city or house divided against itself shall not stand:" (Matt. 12:25)

What standard do Hutterites use to determine that they are the Church of Jesus Christ? According to the written Constitution of the Hutterian Brethren Church, their definition of Jesus' Church is as follows: *"'Church' means the Hutterian Brethren Church and includes all Colonies that adhere to and practice the teachings of the New Testament substantially as expounded by one Peter Rideman as set out in a book or work entitled, 'ACCOUNT*

17

OF OUR RELIGION, DOCTRINE AND FAITH, GIVEN BY PETER RIDEMAN OF THE BROTHERS WHOM MEN CALL HUTTERIANS', and in accordance with the ways of the Hutterian Brethren which includes community of goods, as recognized by the Board of Managers;"

With this definition, the Hutterite Church is combining the Hutterite Constitution with Peter Riedemann's "Confession of Faith," making them both one and the same. Hutterites consider Riedemann one of their most respected forefathers, because his confession details the Hutterite foundational doctrines and beliefs.

Peter Riedemann wrote the original Hutterite interpretation of the Church of Jesus Christ: *"Such a community or church is gathered together by the Holy Spirit, who from then on orders and controls everything in the church. The Spirit leads all the church members to be of one mind and to have one aim, that they might think only like Jesus Christ, and be eager to do his will."* [1]

The Constitution of the Hutterites also states: *"All the members, and especially the Elders, are responsible for carrying out the objects of the Church by following exactly the spontaneous direction of the Holy Spirit and by mutual stimulation and education."*

What noble intentions, certainly attainable. But, as we take a closer look at the present day Hutterian Church, let us see if their aim is truly to *"think only like Jesus Christ, and be eager to do his will,"* [1] and that *"especially the Elders"* are following *"the spontaneous direction of the Holy Spirit."*

Hutterite elders act contrary to the writings of their forefathers when it comes to protecting their own interests, especially when money is involved. They will involve the outside law, go to court, and use the government to do their bidding. All the while every Hutterite minister is required to have Peter Riedemann's writings, which clearly state that a Hutterite is not supposed to go to court even to defend himself.

As we experienced, the Hutterites will go to law without making any biblical efforts toward reconciliation. In a personal account, a leader of a colony went to a lawyer familiar with counseling the Hutterites in the matter of law. The leader was attempting by law to forcefully remove an excommunicated family from the colony premises. The family didn't have the money or physical means to start their new life outside the colony. The family's only offense was that they had biblical beliefs contrary to the Hutterite church's beliefs. How hypocritical! The beliefs for which the family was excommunicated were in total agreement with the Word of God.

Hutterite ministers govern their people contrary to their forefathers' writings. They stand in judgment against those who strive to live a godly life in Christ Jesus. The ministers idolize their forefathers with a sacred reverence, yet they lack the fear of God to follow their full counsel as being led by the Holy Spirit.

The Hutterite leaders take full advantage of the rights and freedoms in the United States and Canada to exert their own will, beliefs, and thinking, many of which are contrary to their forefathers' writings. Hutterite leaders demand the freedom of religion as a shield of defense only to continue with their oppressive regime. Protected by the laws of the above-mentioned governments, Hutterites abuse these laws by withholding the commonly known basic freedoms from individuals, even keeping the knowledge of the existence of such freedoms from colony members.

Outside people don't realize to what great extent Hutterites have been deprived of personal freedoms, and are under the assumption that there is a voluntary surrender of individual rights. Being born into this lifestyle, they might seem to be content, but that is only because they have been trained and conditioned to think, believe, and act like a Hutterite, not knowing there could be another way of life for them. There is no freedom of religion within the confines of their borders. It is a malicious business that will use any means, even religion, to serve its own interests. The strange irony of Hutterite religion is that Hutterite leaders, who cling with fanatical zeal to traditions, quickly compromise their cherished forefathers' beliefs when it involves money.

When one reads Peter Riedemann's book one can only assume that Hutterite leaders must never have read it. The Peter Riedemann book condemns alcohol abuse: *"A congregation made up of sinners-prostitutes, adulterers, rioters, and drunkards; covetous selfish, and vain people; liars in word and deed – is no church of God. Such people do not belong to him."* [1] The serving of alcohol to minors is commonly practiced among Hutterites and is fully condoned by the leaders, who supply the alcohol used in excess. Riedemann wrote strongly against *"public innkeepers, serving wine or beer."* [1] Preachers who are supposed to be an example to those under their care are sometimes the worst offenders. Driving under the influence citations are not unheard of among ministers. Peter Riedemann wrote about priests, *"That priests do not have the Spirit of the Lord is shown by their drunkenness, greed, vanity, pride, swearing, and all kinds of unchastity."* [1]

In a Hutterite wedding, toasting with alcohol is a must, and when someone refused to engage in this custom out of a heartfelt conviction he would often be critized and ridiculed. Here is another quote from Peter Riedemann which once again makes us wonder if the Hutterites, especially the leaders, have ever read the book: *"Drinking toasts is a cause of evil and of disobeying God's commandments. We do not allow it among us because it gives rise to drunkenness, which squanders and destroys both soul and body. You may say that a small drink taken in friendship, since it is enjoyable and desirable, is not wrong. That may be. But we answer that drinking toasts lure a person on to drink when that person would otherwise not do so. Therefore, drinking toasts is unnatural, sinful, and wrong. When persons are not prompted by thirst but are persuaded to drink in order to please others, they transgress God's order and forget about the Creator as well as about their identity."* [1]

By now you might be wondering, "What standard do the Hutterites live by?" We are asking the same question. Obviously, it is not according to the Word of God. It is not even lining up with Peter Riedemann's book. So what does motivate the Hutterite to continue living this communal way of life? Fear cultivated by deception! Even the leaders who propagate this deception, out of self-will and a desire to control others, are themselves victims of fear.

"The God of Israel said, the Rock of Israel spake to me, He that ruleth over men must be just, ruling in the fear of God." (2 Sam. 23:3)

Riedemann wrote about priests: *"If they were servants of the Spirit, they would have the strength and working of the Spirit within themselves, which would tell them that such action would make them slaves, not children. Therefore, they establish only a servile congregation, and slavery has nothing to do with Christ."* [1]

"For they bind heavy burdens and grievous to be borne, and lay them on men's shoulders; but they themselves will not move them with one of their fingers." (Matt. 23:4)

Worship, singing, and prayer are a major part of the Hutterite religion, practiced daily. According to the Hutterite Constitution everything is to be done under the *"spontaneous direction of the Holy Spirit."* The definition of spontaneous in the Webster's dictionary is: *one's free will, voluntary, proceeding from natural feeling or native tendency without external constraint, arising from a momentary impulse, not apparently contrived or manipulated.*

If we didn't grow up as Hutterites we might even believe this to be true, that the Hutterite religion is practiced freely from the heart and is a wonderful spiritual experience. But we did grow up as Hutterites, and boldly declare that the Hutterite church services are dictated, ritualistic, lacking inspiration of the Holy Spirit that refreshes the weary soul. *"Repent ye therefore, and be converted, that your sins may be blotted out, when the times of refreshing shall come from the presence of the Lord."* (Acts 3:19)

There is a yearly repetitive cycle that the Hutterite preachers follow in reading their sermons. They boast that the 400-year-old sermons are "ready cut bread." The Lord's Prayer is, *"give us this day our <u>daily</u> bread."* Hutterite sermons lack this daily revelation borne of the Holy Spirit and are stale. God is constantly doing a new thing; 400-year-old sermons lessen God's perfect will and limit His power in the Church. *"Behold, the former things are come to pass, and new things do I declare: before they spring forth I tell you of them."* (Isa. 42:9)

The Hutterite church services are in German, a language the Hutterites hardly understand. The congregation has no opportunity to speak a syllable in church. The services are so structured that there is no room for personal testimonies, confessions, praise reports, or prayer requests. We were surrounded by a deathly quiet, and one was afraid to even cough or sneeze. The only sound allowed was the preacher's rhythmic reading of the sermon. One could not even bring a Bible to church.

In one of Riedemann's writings he wrote: *"Priests have taken upon themselves the office of proclaiming the gospel, yet they teach only the literal word and the law. They do not have God's strength, namely, the Holy Spirit, which makes a person worthy of such an office."* [1]

Hutterite ministers are not any different than the priests Riedemann condemned.

Hutterites aren't taught to pray from the heart. They pray the same repetitive, memorized prayers for occasions such as mealtime and church. *"But when ye pray, use not vain repetitions, as the heathen do: for they think that they shall be heard for their much speaking."* (Matt. 6:7)

Here is a final excerpt from Peter Riedemann's book: *"In short, a person should cling to God alone. The opposition of this is idolatry. Everything in which one seeks salvation, comfort, or help apart from God, be it in the saints or in anything else created, is idolatry."* [1]

Salvation is found only in Jesus Christ, the Word of God. Has the Hutterite religious system become idolatrous to the Hutterites? Has the Hutterite religion lost the flavor that was established by the godly Hutterite forefathers? *"Ye are the salt of the earth: but if the salt have lost his savour, wherewith shall it be salted? it is thenceforth good for nothing, but to be cast out, and to be trodden under foot of men."* (Matt. 5:13)

Jesus came to expose the works of darkness. He strongly denounced the idolatry and hypocrisy of the Pharisees.

We owe the freedom we enjoy in this country to men and women who did not shrink from conflict but

23

courageously stood against the abuses surrounding them and sought to rectify and bring aright these grievances. The Church of Jesus Christ was founded on the Word of God established in judgment and justice. To bring the standard of the kingdom of God to men everywhere is our aim. *"Of the increase of his government and peace there shall be no end, upon the throne of David, and upon his kingdom, to order it, and to establish it with judgment and with justice from henceforth even for ever. The zeal of the LORD of hosts will perform this."* (Isa. 9:7)

This is not about us and the wrongs we suffered. This is about more than 45,000 Hutterites still living under a system of continual abuse in the United States and Canada. This may also speak to those caught under similar ritualistic religions and denominations.

[16] *"Who will rise up for me against the evildoers? or who will stand up for me against the workers of iniquity?"*

[17] *"Unless the LORD had been my help, my soul had almost dwelt in silence."* (Psa. 94:16-17)

CHAPTER 2

Born Of The Free Woman

Gal. 4:21-31
23 "But he who was of the bondwoman was born after the flesh; but he of the freewoman was by promise."

Sheryl Waldner:
Sheryl left the colony in 2006 at the age of 17. Born in Manitoba, Canada, she currently resides there and operates a prosperous business with her older brother Rodney. She has a passion for waterskiing and has attended a water ski school in Florida. Sheryl loves photography and is moved by God's creation. She also enjoys cooking, swimming, and is learning to play the pan flute and read music. Sheryl has a great love and compassion for people and the business gives her an open door to share the gospel of Jesus Christ with all those who will hear. She is active in a praise and worship flag ministry.

Praise God! He is always faithful to keep His promises as we seek Him with our whole heart and are willing to do what He says. The Word of God says in Heb. 11:6: *"The Lord is a rewarder of those who diligently seek Him."* My Lord and Savior, Jesus Christ, has done so much for me. The testimony He has given me is to glorify Him.

"And ye shall know the truth and the truth shall make you free." (John 8:32)

The way a person believes something to be true depends a great deal on how they were raised. One's heart condition in the moment will determine one's reliance on

God. God is more apt to quickly respond to a soft, teachable heart than to a proud, stubborn-hearted person.

Growing up as a Hutterite until age 17 still affects many of the ways I think, feel, and carry on in life. It takes time to get healing, deliverance and change. The Lord has brought deliverance to me and He is still doing it.

As a Hutterite there are no options for choosing where to work or what career one would envision. Favoritism was a major factor in deciding what was right for one person and not necessarily fair and right for another. My sole task was the assigned colony work. I surrendered and gave up my will, dying inside. There was not a friendly, loving environment, and consequently I talked very little and had no personal ambition. One of the reasons I was so sad was due to the hatred and anger I was exposed to. I remember growing up seeing many arguments, constant gossip, and strife between colony members.

As a little girl I desired to help my Mom when she went to work in the community garden. One warm summer day she let me come and help pick beans. I was thrilled to be included. I was diligently helping to empty the women's pails of fresh picked beans into a bigger box. Suddenly, the garden lady in a fit of anger hollered out for me to go home: "The garden is no place for children." As she ranted on, some of the other women insisted it was okay for me to stay. In the end, the garden lady won and she chased me home. My little heart was crushed. I had done nothing wrong.

With acres of community garden there was an abundance of fruit and vegetables for the community. No one was allowed to freely enter the fruit and vegetable garden to take fresh produce, however. We didn't dare ask the garden managers for permission to take of the overabundance because it was stringently regulated. When my family wanted to eat a few ears of fresh corn at home we had to secretly fumble between the rows of corn in the dark to pick the ears. The ever-ensuing battle over food never ended. There were two long rows of healthy fruit bushes along the garden road that, for a while, the colony members could enjoy whenever they wanted. It was one food source that wasn't canned or sold, but solely for personal enjoyment. One year, for spite, the garden managers agreed to remove the cherry bushes to stop those who might enjoy the fresh fruit at any time. And often at the end of harvest, all the plants with extra produce were hastily plowed under to prevent anyone from picking for their own personal use. The Bible declares that people should have a right to glean the fields after harvest. If gleaning is forbidden, it is unjust and wasteful in the sight of God.

In the community kitchen the main food items were locked up, and at mealtimes the women watched each other jealously to see if anyone took more food than the others. The atmosphere was very tense. There were a lot of arguments over the years stemming from unforgiveness and bitterness that was never resolved in a godly manner.

I was amazed that people who had ill will towards one another could be so friendly and jovial when they were drinking alcohol together. This created a false sense of peace and unity. Alcohol was widely accepted in the colony. Even for those at the young age of 15, alcohol was served at weddings, holidays, and funerals and was virtually free-flowing. The colony leaders regularly distributed alcohol to each individual 15 and over. Being surrounded by these influences at such a young age, it is very rare for any Hutterite man not to drink. There was heavy peer pressure to drink, and it was considered odd to abstain from alcohol. There are many alcoholic Hutterite ministers. And you shouldn't be surprised to know that ministers received

DUIs, some multiple times. Because of this, a flexible rule was made that any minister would be removed from their job after receiving their third DUI. I remember riding home from town with my dad while he was driving under the influence of alcohol. I knew it was illegal because he would hide the alcohol when passing other vehicles. In those moments I didn't care because the alcohol made my dad lighthearted and happy-go-lucky. In my ignorance I viewed alcohol as a good thing because it was so prevalent among the colony members and offered a welcome escape from reality.

What I viewed as normal and right was slanted due to the lack of exposure to the outside world. If we left the colony for a visit it meant going to a different colony, and this was rare. The only time I could go to town would be if my dad had some form of business or I had a doctor's appointment. These trips only lasted a few hours in an afternoon. I was very afraid because I was taught to view any non-Hutterites as the darkened "world." The Hutterites warn you, if you leave and forsake the colony life you will stray from the faith because it is so evil "out there." I was controlled to believe that most outsiders were my enemies. I was terrified to leave my mother's side for fear of being lost, left behind, or forgotten. Also, when visiting other Hutterite colonies I didn't feel safe.

I believed I was better than the outside world because of our "divinely appointed" Hutterite dress code. I was required to wear a traditional Hutterite dress fashioned of one of only two patterns, and at the time I thought this was undeniably vital for my salvation. Our colors were limited, we weren't supposed to wear colors that were too light or too dark, and we could only wear white blouses. When younger, I would fantasize about wearing jeans, pants, and other clothes. When I got older I didn't want to wear anything except the dresses and head covering. I was told the dress and head covering were holy and modest, and nothing could be a better witness of a good submitted Christian woman. What I was told, I believed. Women were commanded to have their heads covered all the time. When I was alone in my room praying and my head wasn't covered, I quickly remembered to obey and would reach for any cloth to put on my head. I felt guilty when praying uncovered, thinking it was unpleasing to God and He wouldn't hear my heart in prayer. I did all of this needlessly. In 1 Corinthians 11:16 Paul states concerning head coverings: *"But if any man seem to be contentious, we have no such custom, neither the churches of God."* What Paul was saying was this issue is not to quarrel over because it is not mandatory for a Christian to participate in this custom. Since I left the colony I can wear what pleases God, without feeling guilty. I will never forget the joy I felt wearing normal "English" clothes for the first time. I can be creative and modest in what I wear. It is so much fun!

So many things the Hutterite leaders would declare had no scriptural basis. We could wear a watch at work, but it was considered unholy in church or at the dining table. When we went to the church or kitchen our head covering had to be tied, and the rest of the time it could be untied. There were many useless religious influences and false teachings that stripped us of our personal freedoms and desensitized our proper judgment. The way it was presented to me at the time, I believed I was being taught the truth, and now realize much of it was heretical teaching. They didn't have a love for the truth, which caused them to believe and teach the lie.

[10] "...because they received not the love of the truth, that they might be saved."

29

[11] "And for this cause God shall send them strong delusion, that they should believe a lie:" (2 Thess. 2:10-11)

The Hutterites speak only the German language in religious ceremonies for they say it is a holy language. Church services were conducted in the German language so it was difficult to know what was being said. We learned just enough German to read and write it to some degree. Hutterites are not even close to being fluent in that language. I understood only bits and pieces. The Hutterites claim their lifestyle and way of living are according to the Word of God. It was all just an outward show. While in church, everyone had a straight somber face and there was no joy or rejoicing. All the men and women wore black jackets; the women sat on one side and the men on the other. It is a rule of order that everyone must be seated according to one's age. There was no life in the singing or preaching. Those in the congregation were not allowed to speak on any subject at any time and only the two ministers would speak. There were no musical instruments and we would only sing old hymns in German. It was all so very stiff and quite stuffy.

The common dialect we spoke was Hutterish. At age five, I began going to school where I learned, to some degree, to understand and speak English. Until I began to learn English, I could only have been influenced by other Hutterites.

We had English school so we could learn to read and write, just enough to get by in an English speaking country. I was far from accomplished in the English language. I was anxious when we had English visitors because they would ask me questions I would have to answer. I couldn't speak fluently in any language. The language barrier was used to keep the people ignorant. In the colony it is okay to say the words "born again" in German. But to say "born again" in

English is viewed as unscriptural. It is obvious the Hutterites don't believe what the Word of God declares in plain and simple English. In some strange way the German language offers some type of safety or security to their lifestyle. The English meaning is very simple and therefore, easily understood. It is offensive to the leaders because it threatens their Hutterite beliefs. Their "holy" language is one more way for them to appear righteous, fully separated from the world and all its ways.

I was not taught about finances, how to write a check, have a bank account, or how to support myself. I didn't know anything about taxes. I didn't know what was happening in the world because we were sheltered from the rest of society and taught there is no need to know what happens in the world. We were not permitted to have a TV or radio.

I was taught that being in school beyond 15 years old was a waste of time. At that age the colony leaders and the members absolutely expected one to work full time for the colony. While in school it felt as though I was part of something important and accepted by my teacher; it felt good to be noticed. I loved the fact that someone was willing to teach and I loved to learn. As I grew older, due to the strong influence from the colony leaders and members, I began to believe the lie that I didn't need an education.

I had watched the negative response from colony members as my brother and his friend graduated from the 12th grade, which very few ever completed. People in the colony said my brother and his friend were lazy and needed to be at work. I never really questioned whether that opinion was right or not. I went along with it because I didn't want to be out of place. I wanted to fit in with everyone else around me and be at peace, but in my heart I was not at peace.

I started my first year of high school at the age of 14. We started teleconferencing as our teachers attempted to teach us over the phone. I was so frozen in fear it affected my mental ability to learn. I felt stupid, thinking I couldn't do the work, and didn't know if I would pass at the end of the year. The way I felt was the direct result of the environment I was in.

I grew up loving school, but after all of this frustration and confusion there was only a glimmer of a desire left to be in school. The greater part of me was overtaken by the influence of the leaders and the people. I felt condemned for taking interest in the normal desire for education. The leaders thought I didn't need further education and pressured me to attend colony work. I had never felt so alone in my life. I had no support and no one to go to in dealing with this paralyzing fear and the hard time I was having emotionally. Before and after school I would pray and read the Word of God to ease my mind. I couldn't apply what I learned in school to colony living. I was very unsettled. In my heart I wanted to go to school, but my head said no. If I had grown up outside of the colony I would have loved to go to school. I would have been encouraged to go to high school and perhaps continue further.

Once I had finished 9th grade I believed I was done with my schooling. I made the obvious choice to be at peace with the inevitable Hutterite ruling. I certainly did not want to be labeled lazy or be the one that would cause others to gossip. I chose to be a good, obedient, responsible Hutterite puppet. I did not want to be in constant fear of peer pressure.

Then, the bomb!

My schoolteacher sat me down and told me I had to continue my schooling. Help me, Lord! Again, confusion and fear instantly rose up inside me. She claimed the colony leaders told her I needed to continue my schooling. How could the leaders demand I continue when schooling was frowned upon all those years? Did the leaders want me to continue until 12th grade and graduate? Was there a change of heart after so many years of ridicule towards a solid education? No. Their reasoning was selfish and deceptive. Here's how I make this claim. The number of students in the colony was deemed to be low and the government would require the colony to pay a percentage for the teacher to continue teaching. I was the number determining if the colony would have to pay or not.

"A false balance is abomination to the LORD: but a just weight is his delight." (Prov. 11:1)

The situation was imbalanced and inconsistent because it was not judged in line with the truth. Nor was it based upon my actions, but rather for the colony's financial gain, proving again that I was just a mere number to satisfy the colony's financial interests. I was caught in the middle. Because of my anxious state it took two difficult years to complete 10th grade. I had become accustomed to feeling incompetent and never measuring up.

My heart is grieved by the spiritual ignorance in the Hutterite colonies and the lack of spiritual discernment for protecting and rearing their children. Every young person entering into puberty will have valid questions concerning the changes in their bodies and there are many easy to understand answers for those questions. When these young bodies begin to change, it can be embarrassing and confusing. I was not taught or shown what was happening to me in the natural progression into adulthood as a young woman experiencing the beginning of the reproductive cycle. I wondered if I had hurt myself, or, in ignorance, I thought I had done something wrong. Shortly after, my Mom did write a letter informing me the changes in my body were normal, but we never talked about it. I needed more understanding, and seeing how ill prepared I was I quickly became more frustrated.

At times, being ignorant of certain facts can be for one's safety and protection, but not in this case. The colony leaders did not allow our public school teacher to teach sexual education. Therefore we were not taught anything on this most important subject. How crazy I was to think if a man put his arm around me, or kissed me, I could become pregnant. This was potentially dangerous and could lead to physical complications that could affect us young people the rest of our lives. These matters require compassionate care and personal attention to avoid such dangers.

Looking back I can see such a vast difference between the colony and "English" lifestyles in helping the young adults to be knowledgeable and safe. Adults should recognize this as a responsible duty to show their children care and respect rather than keeping them in the dark, which may ultimately open doors to unhealthy sexual practices.

Along with many others, I was a victim of the sexual abuse that happens so often in the colony. There was no one that really knew what was going on or to protect me. Those that suspected something was wrong wouldn't do anything about it. We were on our own. These hidden things caused spiritual and emotional scars. As I got older I discerned the same abuse was happening to another child and I warned the parent, but the parent would not listen. My genuine concern was rejected by a mocking dismissal. Thinking it was not serious enough, the parent turned a blind eye. Situations such as this happen and are ignored, leaving victims within a "let's keep it quiet" and "it'll be all right" secrecy. After I left the colony I received healing through Jesus Christ and godly counsel from true servants of the Lord.

It is shocking to me to know that the Hutterites think they can do whatever they want and believe they are above the law. Hutterites believe they can adequately handle matters of child abuse without reporting to the outside authorities. They "handle" it with little or no counsel for either the victim or the guilty person. They believe whatever they decide is right and how they operate is the ultimate standard, when in reality it is not the standard of the Word of God. The fact that children are abused is kept quiet and swept under the rug.

Hutterite leaders and parents turn a blind eye to legitimate problems within the colony. But, when someone boldly confesses their faith in the Lord Jesus Christ this news swiftly spreads throughout the colonies. An avalanche of gossip runs rampant about this simple basic truth of the gospel of Jesus Christ. Feeling threatened, Hutterites resist the conviction of the Holy Spirit for their own lives. Hutterite colony ministers are pressured by the Hutterite committee of elders to take a stand against anyone being "born again." If they believe in salvation according to the Word of God and boldly confess the name of Jesus, they risk losing their position as a Hutterite preacher. The Bible clearly states we must be saved and born again to see and enter the kingdom of God.

"Jesus answered and said unto him, Verily, verily, I say unto thee, Except a man be born again, he cannot see the kingdom of God." (John 3:3)

My surroundings affected every aspect of who I was and how I was living. Because the ministers didn't teach me about salvation through Jesus Christ, I couldn't understand the Word of God or how to follow Jesus Christ. I didn't see how I could be used of God or needed by anyone. I could not hear God's voice. I didn't know who I was, what I was doing, or why Jesus created me. I didn't have confidence, and constantly felt condemned. I was alone without Jesus.

This hopelessness left me weak and faint-hearted. I was intimidated and wondered what everyone thought of me. I often wondered, "Am I working hard enough to please anyone and will I be noticed?" If someone was sick or weaker than the rest in any way, they would become a victim of condemning gossip. We would try to follow the many ordinances and get approval from the leaders and the rest of the colony people. The colony was not a peaceful, safe place where people could be real and open. No one's heartfelt desire, concern, or vision mattered, which resulted in isolation. I grew up where it didn't matter how I felt or how I was doing emotionally. It took a while after I left the colony to identify my emotions and realize the things in my heart were important to others as well as myself.

The first time I heard about salvation in Jesus Christ was when an ex-Hutterite came to visit and teach the Word of God, focusing on salvation in Jesus Christ. This was the first time salvation was explained to me. It was exciting news to say the least. I wanted it, but it was so hard to believe I could simply say a prayer and get saved. I went home and prayed with all my heart. I asked Jesus to come into my heart and asked Him to forgive me all the wrong I had done.

The Holy Spirit started convicting me of my sins and drawing me closer to the truth. Yet, I had a constant struggle with having assurance of salvation. It was difficult to accept Jesus' forgiveness for my sins. Because I had no one to help me it took years of struggle before I was assured of my salvation. In the typical Hutterite mindset one is accepted by their good behavior and works and it's impossible to know if one is saved. A Hutterite's only hope for heaven is to be faithful to the colony's way of living till the end. This belief is contrary to the truth in the Word of God. Salvation only comes by grace through faith in Jesus Christ. *"Not of works, lest any man should boast."* (Eph. 2:8-9)

"These things have I written unto you that believe on the name of the Son of God; that ye may <u>know</u> that ye have eternal life, and that ye may believe on the name of the Son of God." (1 John 5:13)

I had a God-given desire to associate with other believers in Christ Jesus, but didn't have the liberty to leave the colony and go where I could worship freely. I wanted to be with Christians, not only some that were Hutterites, but also believers that were "English." Months later the same ex-Hutterite who had come to our home and preached about salvation was going to be in the nearest town with other believers in Jesus Christ. My siblings, cousins, and I wanted to hear more about Jesus, a Jesus who was real and personal. I was stirred and hungered for more. I really wanted to visit them, but I knew this wouldn't be allowed by the colony preacher. We asked my dad if we could secretly use his vehicle, but he didn't want us to. Finally, my brother just took it. We were too desperate to care about the consequences. The Bible study was encouraging and refreshing. We received personal prayer, something I had never experienced before as a Hutterite. There was no doubt in my mind we did the right thing.

The colony preacher found out and told my dad, the German schoolteacher, to punish us. The customary method of punishment for unbaptized teenagers was to stand during the Sunday school lesson, apologize, and then receive a strict lecture. Thankfully, my Dad avoided the order to punish us. In a different instance, there was a songfest in another colony with a bunch of young people getting together who confessed Jesus as their Savior. We knew we needed some excuse to get a vehicle and leave the colony so we could attend the songfest. We told the preacher we wanted to donate blood at the nearest town and afterwards go to this certain colony where the songfest was being held. As soon as the preacher heard the name of that colony he strictly forbade us to go there. The colony preacher allowed us to go donate blood but ordered us to visit a different colony where no one would profess to be saved in the name of Jesus Christ. His refusal was heartbreaking and very disappointing. The God-given desire and conviction inside of us drove us to the desperate measure to sneak away and attend the meeting anyway.

The Lord created every human being with a free will to choose according to their conscience. By this, we have the right and ability to know what God is saying to us so we may follow and obey Him.

When I cried out to God with all my heart for help, he delivered me. Praise God! I couldn't find what I needed until I had left the colony. The Lord God Almighty led me to a small group that loved the Lord with all their heart and they proved it by their love one to another. They were firmly established on the Word of God and preached everything that pertains to life and godliness. *"For I have not shunned to declare unto you all the counsel of God."* (Acts 20:27) Since I committed to discipleship His purposes are being fulfilled in my life.

I am in a safe place where I am free to share my heart and have value and worth. When we assemble for prayer and teaching of the Word of God, everyone who is present is involved. I have an abundant life in Jesus Christ because He lives in me. I hear the voice of God and I can do exactly what He tells me to do. It is truly amazing what God does with us humans when we surrender to the Lord Jesus Christ.

I had no idea there was so much to see and do in obedience to the still small voice of God. God values each individual on the earth. Every person is uniquely created by God with specific giftings, and it is up to us individually to learn what these are and exercise them in a walk of faith. And in that day I don't want to say unto the Lord I was in a place where I couldn't or wouldn't do what He was commanding me to do.

A few days after I left the colony I desperately wanted to be water baptized. I was now assured of my salvation in Jesus Christ and wanted to obey Jesus' command to be water baptized.

"He that believeth and is baptized shall be saved..." (Mark 16:16)

The joy I experienced is real and available for all those who believe and are baptized. It was true peace and liberty that moved me to rejoice from my heart when I experienced how simple it is. I wasn't asked about my age, or to wait for a certain time of year, or to memorize someone else's testimony. Being Hutterite, I would have been required to perform these and other customs, which I didn't understand and could not give proof of my heart's dedication to God. I confessed my personal faith in Jesus Christ and dedicated my life to Him. My heart being right toward God is the only thing that mattered.

The Lord has blessed me to have my own business where I have learned about customer relations, advertising, and quality of character. I earn money, pay taxes, pay bills, have a home, and have the liberty to boldly preach the Word of God. Now I have a driver's license, which as a woman in the colony I was not allowed. Having learned that people outside the colony are not the enemy, it is fulfilling and brings great joy to meet and serve people. The Lord has afforded me the ability to support myself and loads me daily with His benefits. As I delight myself in the Lord, His desires become mine so I work through God's grace and power to glorify God in whatever I do.

[3] "Trust in the LORD, and do good; so shalt thou dwell in the land, and verily thou shalt be fed."

[4] "Delight thyself also in the LORD; and he shall give thee the desires of thine heart." (Psa. 37:3-4)

Insecurities and lack of personal social worth are things I had to deal with for some time after I left the colony. Hutterite women are more suppressed than the men. A Hutterite woman can't speak out or lead in any way without the men essentially controlling everything a woman may do. Once I overcame the lie that I was incapable, it was so much fun learning basic things and experiencing life to the fullest. I am a capable woman with as much worth to God as a man.

"There is neither Jew nor Greek, there is neither bond nor free, there is neither male nor female: for ye are all one in Christ Jesus." (Gal. 3:28)

I have been privileged by God to visit many different places in the United States and see so many wonderful things God created for our eyes to see. I saw the ocean, the mountains, and flew in airplanes. I have learned how to swim and water ski. These may seem like minor things to some, but to me they are miracles. It is so refreshing just being able to be at peace, sitting at a campfire exhausted from waterskiing and enjoying the sunset at the lake. I am thankful unto the Lord for how He blesses His people. I've been to a musical symphony. I'm learning to play the pan flute and I enjoy worshipping the Lord in dance. It has brought deliverance and breakthrough in my life. God is faithful and has given me exceedingly, abundantly above what I could ever ask or think. He has provided me with a professional, high quality camera, thus fulfilling a vision I had of blessing others in capturing God's creation. What a blessing to enjoy God's beauty and worship Him in freedom and not anticipate who might attempt to condemn me.

Everyone that is saved, born again, has the command to share the gospel. If one declares they are a Christian they should willingly obey the Word of God. Why is it, the Hutterites claim to be Christians, and yet, they don't evangelize? *"As you go, preach, saying the kingdom of heaven is at hand."* (Matt. 10:7) The Hutterites are closed off and don't welcome newcomers. I have only heard of two converts won over to Hutterism. The Hutterites believe no one will ever be as holy and privileged as those born Hutterite. Therefore, if there is to be any growth in numbers it will only be done from the inside.

Why don't the Hutterites obey Jesus' command to preach the gospel to the lost? In Isaiah 52:7 it says: *"How beautiful upon the mountains are the feet of him that bringeth good tidings, that publisheth peace; that bringeth good tidings of good, that publisheth salvation; that saith unto Zion, Thy God reigneth!"*

Man's traditions cannot overrule the power in the truth of the Word of God. The Hutterite ministers and teachers ignore the spiritual condition of the people that are dying, hurting, and needing to hear the Word of God and experience the love of Jesus.

Since I have left the colony I have been blessed by God to be able to work where I meet many people and have had opportunity to share Jesus with them. We pray together, share the scriptures, and have fellowship one with another. The Word of God commands us to humble ourselves, love one another, care for others and put their needs above our own to have any effect to the glory of God.

Hutterites don't understand salvation by faith in Jesus Christ through repentance, believing, and confession, therefore the Hutterites can't share salvation with someone in need. One can't give what they don't have. What a sorrowful state of heart! For there is so much joy in knowing Jesus and sharing His love with others. Only because of His grace and my deep yearning for the truth in the Word of God did I surrender to the Lord and commit to be His disciple. And all this to the glory of God, the Lord Jesus set me free!

Let's say I have a greenhouse full of plants that need fertilizer. Someone gives me a substandard product, which causes them to not produce any fruit. Trusting the person who gave me the product, I keep using it, hoping in time it would do good. But because I continue using the substandard product the plants produce nothing and start to die.

Trying to be a Christian and a Hutterite is similar. Some know they are dying spiritually, yet they stay in the colony. Many are constantly looking over their shoulders and wondering what others will think of them if they leave the colony. Some have thought, "Maybe I will leave next year" or, "If I stay, maybe it will get better."

As a Hutterite you don't have the freedom to talk about Jesus, or go where God is leading you. You can't associate freely with other Christians. As a Hutterite you won't get discipled or regularly encouraged. You won't be able to fulfill God's calling for you. If God called you to minister to people away from the colony you could not go. If God had told me to immediately go to the city hospital to pray for a person's healing, it would have been impossible.

I am not saying these things because I am against anyone. It is to tell those who are in bondage they can be set free by the Lord Jesus Christ. I am writing these things out of love. I love everyone and I have no unforgiveness or

42

animosity toward anyone, anywhere. I see how a religious system that is out of godly order can crush an individual.

Thank you, my Lord and Savior Jesus Christ, for without Your grace and love toward me, I'd still be miserable and lost…

Thank you, Jesus!

CHAPTER 3

I Wanted It, I Got It: Life, Liberty And The Pursuit Of Happiness.

Karen Waldner:
Karen was born in Manitoba, Canada. She grew up under the Hutterite culture. Karen lived there until 2006 when she left at the age of 20. Her parents were forced to leave the colony for taking a stand for Christian, biblical beliefs. Currently, all her family has left the colony. Karen is now happily married to Jason Waldner and is enjoying a peaceful home-life in the United States. She is now successful in business and is actively pursuing an interest in interior design. She enjoys calligraphy, arts and crafts, waterskiing, travel, and occasionally working with her husband in carpentry. Karen is a team leader in a choreographed dance praise and worship group.

It has been six years … six of the most exciting and eventful, yet challenging, years of my life. Within those years I received my U.S. citizenship, making me a dual citizen of the United States and Canada. I moved to the United States to establish a walk with Jesus Christ through intense biblically-based discipleship. While being discipled I met Jason, a brother in the Lord. After nearly a year of discipleship God drew us together, and months later I was blessed to call him my husband.

Now, being afforded the time and opportunity to study the U.S. Constitution and the Declaration of Independence, I can't help but praise the Lord who gave me such freedom wherein I can serve Him freely with my wholehearted devotion. I now have:

- The freedom to worship God from the heart

- The freedom to fellowship with likeminded believers of any nation, people, and tongue (Rev. 5:9)

- A place where I have personal rights and freedoms secured by law

- A place I call home

- A freedom to choose a career with God's direction

In the United States Declaration of Independence it states, *"We hold these truths to be self-evident, that all men are created equal, that they are endowed by their Creator with certain unalienable Rights, that among them are Life, Liberty and the pursuit of Happiness."* The Canadian Charter of Rights also clearly states the fundamental freedoms that people are entitled to have and enjoy. In North Dakota, where I now live, the Constitution states in Sect. 1, *"All individuals are by nature equally free and independent…"*

Here I find a drastic difference between these documents of individual freedoms and liberty, and that of the Hutterite constitution under which I lived for 20 years. When I was living under the Hutterite church government such rights and privileges were not available to me.

The Hutterite constitution Article 3(b) states: *"Complete dedication in the work for the aims and objects of the Church is expected from all Colonies and their members."*

Article 40: *"Each and every member of a Colony shall give and devote all his or her time, labour, services, earnings and energies to that Colony, and the purposes for which it is formed, freely, voluntarily and without compensation or reward of any kind whatsoever, other than herein expressed."*

I understand the basic rights and freedoms, especially the freedom of religion, granted in the United States and Canada. What baffles me is how the Hutterites use these basic rights to nullify the individual's God-given freedom and expect everything from their members, *"...all of his or her time, labour, services, earnings and energies..."* There are no such required demands of extreme devotion to any state or government entities within the documents of liberty for the people in the United States or Canada.

Now I understand why I felt such separation between myself and the people on the outside of the colony. The "outside English" lived under a constitution of religious freedoms. I was living under a Hutterite religious constitution that kept me enslaved to man's rules and regulations, which are contrary to the freedoms that God's Word of Truth offers all people.

The Hutterites have a secluded, communistic way of life. The Hutterite woman's dress code and the Hutterite language are two very obvious stumbling blocks that kept me from relating to the outside world. As a Hutterite woman, I didn't realize there could ever be any opportunity for me to associate with people from the "outside." The outside world views the Hutterite women to be so different and somehow mysterious. The outsiders would keep their distance from the Hutterites and the Hutterites from them. When I went into a business or a grocery store, I would avoid speaking to them as much as possible. My mother would speak for me in most situations. How could I ever evangelize and boldly preach the gospel of Jesus Christ as the Word of God commands in Mark 16:15: *"Go ye into all the world, and preach the gospel to every creature."* It was virtually impossible. But why don't the Hutterites keep Jesus' command to preach in His name His gospel to all people, everywhere?

I wasn't taught how to evangelize or reach out to people. If I had an opportunity to witness or evangelize it wouldn't be effective because all of our religious instructions were in the German language. Consequently, I couldn't be obedient to Jesus' command.

The German Bible is the only Bible sanctioned by the Hutterite Church. How could the Word of God in German lead an English speaking person to Jesus? I didn't understand the German language enough to apply it to my life, nor did I know the English Bible to preach it to others. Therefore, I kept quiet about God and His Word. Finally, the day came when I was blessed to get a Bible that was printed in English. The scriptures were as if God lit them up just for me to see and understand. I was excited and encouraged to read and study my Bible. It was hard to put it down. I was torn between wanting to stay at home and rejoice as I devoured the scriptures or go to church only to hear the 400 year old, worn out German sermons over and over again. We were not permitted to bring any Bible to church. I wanted, I needed fresh revelation from the Throne of Grace for my life. In the half hour or the one hour services the monotone delivery was lulling me into a spiritual sleepiness. I realize now, I was kept unaware, ignorant, and ill-equipped concerning life. I should have had the truth many years before this.

I grew up hearing that anything outside the Hutterite way of life was called "the world." Everything non-Hutterite was considered worldly, therefore they deem themselves righteous, and without checks and balances an attitude of superiority and self-righteousness confronts "the world."

True Christianity, with Jesus as the head, is to have love for God and one another. A type of "Christianity" that is focused and growing only within their own community lifestyle is not true Christianity. Little did I know that someday I would be free from this spiritual bondage. I was under a cloud of hopelessness and fear. I was weary from working with contentious women and mountains of dissatisfaction. Dissatisfaction breeds dissatisfaction. I was trapped. I decided, this is going to end and I will not continue living this way. I saw how I was closed off from all society without an education or understanding for how to survive on the outside. It seemed impossible to leave. Where would I live? Could I find a job? Will I have friends?

I was dying in the colony and this was not the place for me to die. With deep conviction and desperation my heart cried out, "I'm leaving, no matter what the cost!" In Jesus' words: (Luke 12:50 Amplified) *"...how greatly and sorely I am urged on (impelled, constrained) until it is accomplished."*

I sought the Lord for help and truth in my life. While in the colony I couldn't serve God freely or confess Jesus' name openly. God opened the door for me to leave and I knew if I stayed in the colony I would be in disobedience and rebellion, always falling short of doing God's perfect will. So, I submitted to God and left once and for all. I have never looked back or regretted it for a second.

God divinely intervened and led me to a place He had prepared for me. Godly leadership was there for me personally and taught me how to hear from God, follow and serve Jesus Christ. I was taught how to love God and people. What God promised in Jeremiah 3:14-15 was truly fulfilled.

[14] *"...and I will take you one of a city, and two of a family, and I will bring you to Zion:"*

[15] *"And I will give you pastors according to mine heart, which shall feed you with knowledge and understanding."*

The basic things in everyday life others may take for granted, I now see as awesome opportunities for me. The right to earn money, go shopping, buy groceries, eat out at restaurants, and take vacations, are just a few of these opportunities of a regular lifestyle of freedom. Acquiring my driver's license was a milestone for me. I saw it as a welcome advancement into normal society. I couldn't stop smiling when I passed my driving test.

I say all this to bring to light the deception that kept me from living a life of freedom. Many people see the Hutterites as "one big happy family." Yet, the Hutterite form of society erodes the very foundation of family life. For example, children eat all three meals in the children's dining room. The parents are separated to a dining hall with adult men and women. Having a family supper was a real treat but this only took place a few times a year. Why couldn't my parents sit together with me and my siblings? Was I wrong in wanting to do this? Not even my parents as husband and wife could share a meal together or sit together at church services. I certainly do have a righteous anger toward that type of religious, emotional, and monetary control over someone's basic freedoms as a human being. The Word of God declares, in a Christian family the parents are responsible to raise and discipline their own children as they see fit. But, contrary to God's order, my German schoolteacher had to discipline and lecture the children. Instead of telling my parents about an offense, it was dealt with in German class or at the breakfast, lunch, or dinner meal times. My parents weren't consulted or informed about most of these punishments. My parents had to go along with the system, being kept ignorant of the order God ordained for parents and children. *"And, ye fathers provoke not your children to wrath: but bring them up in the nurture and admonition of the Lord."* (Eph. 6:4)

God primarily holds parents responsible for the upbringing of children, not grandparents, not schools, nor peers or friends. Although each of these groups may influence children, the final duty rests with the parents and, ultimately, the father whom God has appointed as the "head" to lead and serve the family. Instead, I was raised in an atmosphere of condemnation, intimidation, and fear, which will "provoke a child to wrath." I know how impersonal and secluded this life can be ... I lived it for 20 years. I don't remember my parents giving me a hug and saying, "I love you" in the colony. I rarely received encouragement from my parents or anyone else.

Can you imagine a woman starting a menstrual cycle without expecting it or having any understanding of what was happening to her? I was frightened and much too embarrassed to ask questions. I thought I had a serious sickness. Months went by before my Mom approached me with female products and a short explanation how to use them, and walked away. I still didn't realize that all women my age experience this natural event in their life. Just knowing this would have been a relief! I wasn't taught the basic common sense knowledge of my body, so it was hard to know what questions to ask.

A few years later, when my brothers were out of the house, five of us young girls got together and opened up to

51

one another about our experiences becoming women on our path to adulthood. We stayed up past midnight, talking. I found out my older sisters had similar experiences. One sister thought it was caused by a hard fall. She tried to cure it with vitamins and other home remedies. When it stopped she tried to identify which remedy worked. The other sister quit riding a bicycle because she thought that's what caused it. After that evening we felt so relieved and excited to finally know we were normal.

My mother and three of her sisters had nine daughters among them of similar age. It bewilders me to think they would not confer amongst themselves to establish these basic needs for their daughters. Why was it so shameful for them to talk about the reproductive cycle or childbearing, which is one of the main responsibilities of a Hutterite woman? We were raised to view these matters as private and not to be discussed, even with my mother, so I never dared talk with her.

It is wise and safe for parents to continue to teach the children common sense instruction as they mature in everyday life. My mother was never taught to communicate effectively on those real heartfelt issues.

After I left the Hutterite colony I received the care and instruction I desperately needed to become a confident and mature woman of God, and to someday teach others. I finally experienced the positive alternative to the fear and secrecy through a godly example. They were rich in encouragement, and patient as they listened with love and affection.

The colony I grew up in was known for its strife and hatred, which had begun in past generations. It was between relatives who were constantly fighting amongst themselves. This generational friction was passed down to the next generation. There were numerous instances where the grandparents' unresolved conflicts came down upon the parents and I witnessed this being passed to us, the children. Other ministers attempted to help end the conflicts but never brought any resolution. My father and his two brothers lived in the same colony for years and the three together rarely ever saw eye to eye. I'm still not sure why and I never saw any attempts at a resolution. They just weren't close. To this day they all attend different churches and all of this after nearly 50 years of living as Hutterite "Christians." The "world" has more understanding and proof of close, binding, and loving relationships than in the legalistic Hutterite church.

The struggles to have positions of authority caused great competitive jealousy. When someone was put into a leadership position, they and their families would reap benefits. They would have access to food that was locked up and portioned medical supplies. When making phone calls to anyone outside our colony there was a time restriction of 10 to 15 minutes. If the call was during the day, access had to be granted by the leader. These phone calls also came with a 10 to 15 minute restriction and the leader and his family could listen to our phone conversation. So much for Acts 4:32, the scripture the Hutterites base their faith on: *"And the multitude of them that believed were of one heart and of one soul: neither said any of them that ought of the things which he possessed was his own; but they had all things common."*

According to the Hutterite constitution, I couldn't have, nor did I have any possessions. I couldn't freely give of my own because I was a slave to the system. In the book of Acts, people had their own houses and possessions, and they freely shared and never "said" these things were their own. The colony life forcefully takes; nothing is freely given. It has been said, "If everybody would get their share, the Hutterite church would fall apart because most people would leave." This fact strikes fear into the hearts and minds of the Hutterite leaders, for they know people's hearts are not loyal towards the system and their fellow man. Therefore the leaders keep the colony members in religious bondage and control them with the money, time, transportation, personal aspirations, etc.

Individuals in the colony work all their lives without a salary or paycheck. The colony as a business organization generates a sizable income by the combined efforts of those who work in the colony. The secretary files taxes on behalf of an individual who is of legal tax paying age. The secretary applies falsified income to the individual that is in fact part of the colony income. The amount of income claimed in the person's tax report is well hidden from that person. While the colony benefits, the government receives a falsified report of personal income, when in all honesty, truth, and reality the person only received $3.00 or $5.00 per month. The colony leadership takes the unfounded liberty to use the colony member's name and establish numbers and falsified communications with the government entities without the colony member's knowledge or full consent. Unsuspecting individuals are ultimately faced with obeying the leader's demands or leave the colony with little to nothing.

When my sister and I left the colony, our dad, who was excommunicated, helped us file our tax returns. We expected to receive a refund since we had no income that year. Much to our surprise, we were not only denied a refund but also had to pay taxes on income we never even received. This was due to the colony income that was recorded under our names. We found ourselves legally indebted to the government for a personal tax bill. We did not know our names and numbers were used. When my brother had a similar experience he attempted to get sensible answers from the colony secretary to satisfy his debt. He was refused. The guilty secretary made excuses and would not agree to pay this debt that was fictitiously produced. Our Dad paid the tax on the money that was declared under our names. The colony richly benefited from our hard labors and kept the income. Without conscience they burdened us with an unjust tax debt and robbed us of the opportunity to receive the much needed refund.

I praise the Lord for allowing me to leave the colony and live in a country where men and women stand up and fight so we can enjoy those God-given freedoms listed in the Declaration of Independence and the Constitution. I have learned how those courageous men and women boldly stood for freedom. I choose to stand with God to establish and strengthen the liberties for those who are the oppressed and suffer wrongfully at the hands of unjust judges and counselors.

CHAPTER 4

And Then... The Day Star Arose In My Heart.

2 Peter 1:19
"We have also a more sure word of prophecy; whereunto ye do well that ye take heed, as unto a light that shineth in a dark place, until the day dawn, and the day star arise in your hearts:"

Rodney Waldner:

Rodney enjoys mechanical work on cars, trucks, and working on his own competition water ski boat. He enjoys slalom and trick skiing, and is a skilled boat driver. He can design and construct wood and metal projects for home and his construction business. He loves farming and carpentry. Rodney enjoys music, attending the symphony, and loves to play the drums. Rodney left the colony life in deep depression and couldn't find help after attending various ministries and Bible schools. He discovered a ministry in the United States and to God be all the glory he is now fully delivered and serving the Lord Jesus Christ with joy and freedom. He operates a business with his sister Sheryl in Manitoba, Canada where he resides.

Walk with me, if you will, as we go down a road where I will plainly describe a part of my life as a Hutterite. I lived it, grew up in it, and experienced it firsthand.

When we are young we follow what we see and what we are taught, and continue in what we believe as true. As I grew older and observed my experiences, I began to question my own actions and habits. It is wise and healthy to question if the very standards that are imposed upon human beings do not make sense, due to double standards by man's rules or traditions that ultimately create confusion and dissention.

The human race is always adapting to creative change. Some folks don't accept change if or when it comes, even when it is absolutely necessary. What happens when the truth arises and there is a resounding fervor for change and we don't move? We as individuals, and society as a whole, could be put at peril and the consequences could become catastrophic. In some situations, unless we remove ourselves physically, we cannot truly discern what is happening. I urge you to hear the cry of a heart that understands from personal experience what it's like inside a Hutterite colony.

One may say, as they read this, "Stop feeling sorry for yourself" or "Most children go through these similar situations." I understand. But when a religious community twists scriptures from the Word of God in such a way to deceive and manipulate great numbers of unwary people, then those lies and deceptions must be exposed.

As my personal God-given responsibility I speak to those who are enslaved by these subtle forms of entrapment. There are many hurting people within religious systems who deserve to hear and know the truth.

The Hutterite system is tolerated in society. Most people have no idea what truly goes on inside the colonies because everything is so secretive. This is a perfect environment for hidden agendas. By boldly standing and speaking the truth in love, God's wonderful purpose for those bound by lies can come to full fruitfulness and prosperity in Jesus Christ. I gladly share the wondrous deliverance God has wrought for me.

In the colony there was little care or concern for my body, soul, or spirit. I was kept ignorant and don't remember receiving godly counsel for my life or future. I didn't experience a sincere heartfelt interest or godly concern being shown towards one another within the Hutterite groupings. To this day my heart goes out to those who suffer this neglect and are left without direction or way of escape.

The leaders are quite content to keep the people in the system functioning in a state of robotic ignorance. I experienced living in a place that receives blanket protection as a religious organization, thus avoiding having to pay wages, comply with child labor laws, and follow safety measures. And yet, they are clearly running a commercial operation no different than any business or factory outside of the colony. Which business in the United States or Canada could get away without paying wages to their workers or having proper safety measures? Why do Hutterites have these exclusive privileges? The colony as an entity owns everything in the colony: houses, vehicles, lands, money, businesses, etc. Members are not allowed to own anything. My daily purpose was all about upholding Hutterite traditions and making money for the colony. I understand making money, I have nothing against it, but hiding behind a cloak of religion is wrong.

I recall how the colony took the elderly's government pension checks and boasted that those checks paid for most of the groceries for everyone in the colony. Imagine working all your life in the colony and all you ever get is a few measly dollars a month for an allowance. I recall a number of reoccurring shameful and degrading actions toward an elderly man who had medical appointments and had need of money for travel expenses. This gentleman went to ask for money from the colony secretary. At times he would get a mere $20.00. As the gossip rumble began I heard the secretary was complaining that the elderly man was coming too often to ask for money. He was given the money, but begrudgingly. It was like using a giant crowbar to pry open the purse. What happened to taking care of the elderly? Especially when the elderly's pension checks, according to the leader, were used to feed most of the colony members! Why would leaders resentfully give money for bare necessities, especially to the elders, who had loyally worked for the colony the longest? Living in the colony was for everybody to have all things common with all their needs met. Obviously, the money wasn't for everyone equally. The leaders have all the money, credit cards, check books, vehicles, and access to almost everything. They use this to exercise their control over unwary and innocent people.

There are times in my life when I ponder what really happened to me in those years of colony life. Sometimes it's easier not to remember. Then, I think how selfish it would be for me not to share my knowledge and experience. There are people out there who have had and are now going through similar situations.

Throughout the years of my life as a Hutterite I saw much preferential treatment. My friends and I liked going to the nearest city to attend semi-pro hockey games, which was against the colony rules. It was one of the only fun highlights we had and we felt guilty most of the time for it. We always had to look over our shoulder for the ones who might be watching us. Fortunately for us, my dad was the manager of the chicken barn and we would have him arrange feed pickups with a colony truck on days when there were scheduled hockey games. Otherwise, out of desperation we would just take a vehicle (which was pretty much considered stealing) or we would get a ride from the local postmaster. I used to go pick up feed with the leader's son, whom I worked with in the chicken and turkey barn. It was a well-oiled plan until the leader's son was given a different work position and I was responsible for picking up feed in town. I wanted my dad to continue scheduling feed pickups on hockey nights. It worked for a short time until my dad was confronted by the leader and ordered to stop us. Out of fear my dad listened to the leader and purposely set feed pickups when there were no games scheduled. It's a funny thing; I have gone to some of the games since I left the colony and saw at least one of that leader's sons at the game, every time I went.

I was about eight years of age when I was riding along with a friend who had just gotten the responsibility of operating a new riding lawn mower. A member of the colony came up to us, stopped us and in an angry manner said, "Why do you have the mower?" I was scared as I sat frozen next to my friend. We soon realized he wanted his son to have the responsibility of the new mower. Through a pecking order the time finally came that I was given the responsibility to use and take care of the mower. I anticipated there would be a day I would be approached by an elder, and sure enough that day came. I was asked the same question. "Why do you have the mower and why didn't my grandson get it since he's older than you?" I was scared. I didn't know what to say. I stood up, dug in my heels, and mustered up the courage to defend my mighty domain of taking care of a single lawnmower. It was typical for the leaders to avoid ironing out these problems amongst themselves. As you can see, I was surrounded by much bitterness and strife.

The leaders' sons were entrusted with tractors to drive and maintain at ages 14 and 15. Others like me who didn't have a dad as a colony leader would have to wait several years longer. As a teenager it was difficult because I wanted the opportunity to prove myself responsible and trustworthy. I struggled when I saw the younger boys getting to drive tractors and swathers. My mind was wildly racing with questions. I wondered over and over if I was stupid, incapable, and worthless. Finally at the age of 21, one of the younger men made it his mission to give me the responsibility of driving a grain swather. As I sat in "my" swather, which I kept spotless, I finally felt some sense of worth. But sure enough, one of the leaders complained and wanted his 15-year-old son to drive the swather instead of me. There is an attitude of superiority maintained by the leaders and their families, believing they have an edge on everyone and everything, everywhere.

James 3:16-17 declares, *"For where envying and strife is there is confusion and every evil work. But the wisdom that is from above is first pure, then peaceable, gentle and easy to be intreated, full of mercy and good fruits, without partiality, and without hypocrisy."*

The system creates the necessity for self-survival and man-pleasing accomplishment. Everyone was out for himself. In my heart I knew there was more to life than what was presented to me as a Hutterite. It is not the will of God to have innocent people cooped up in a mental prison. There is a way to live without contention and hostility. The true love of God transcends all of those mean and vindictive attitudes.

What a child sees, hears, learns and experiences is very important. One can be scarred for life with dramatic effects, mentally, physically and emotionally. There are essentially no safety measures taught or practiced in the colony. This creates very dangerous circumstances for all people in the colony, especially the young children.

Here are a few accounts from my personal experiences to verify the complete absence of safety in the day-to-day life in a colony.

When I was three years old I was riding on a trailer behind a tractor my Dad was driving. I was playing with a stick and leaned over the trailer to hold the stick against the wheel. I fell off the trailer and the trailer wheel ran over my head causing severe injury. There was gravel imbedded into my scalp and part of my ear was torn off, leaving permanent damage to my scalp and ear.

When I was seven I was working in the chicken barn with thousands of chickens, doing chores. I was working at the machine that automatically feeds the chickens. I was maintaining the machine by clearing feed from around the main drive wheel, when suddenly my hand was drawn between the cable and the drive pulley, which severed part of my finger.

Less than a year later, nearing the end of the English school year, I was helping to burn old schoolwork and textbooks in a trash barrel beside the school. The teacher brought a can of gas to the fire. When I poured the gas on the fire some of it splashed onto my pant leg and ignited. I panicked and frantically fought to tear my pants off. By the time I got my pants off I had suffered third degree burns.

The gross negligence and careless disregard for safety standards proved to have a demoralizing effect upon my life. Instead of being a carefree young child full of adventure I felt unsafe and unprotected. I became withdrawn, self-conscious, and fearful. I was constantly aware and ashamed of my loss and disfigurement.

While in school I was required to attend a first aid class in a nearby town. When I asked the minister/secretary for permission to go, he said, "It's not important. Stay home and shovel manure." He told me I was not allowed to go.

My dad intervened and called the minister to tell him I was going to that class. He stood his ground knowing the class was essential and mandatory.

As a teenager I realized I needed more education than the 9th and 10th grade that the colony deemed as sufficient. Colony work had unquestioned priority over education. Dropping out of school before 10th grade is what most everyone did in the colony where I grew up. What we learned of the English language in all our classes was minimal. There was very little accountability from the school division, parents, or leaders in the colony. Very little effort was required to complete the studies because of a lax textbook study structure and weak lesson plans. There was too much free time and precious hours were squandered away watching movies. Of course watching movies was only allowed in school. We also played computer games, bingo, and certain games outside. Homework was hardly ever assigned. It is not the child's responsibility to make sure they are learning what they need in order to function in society outside the colony.

The classroom was pretty crazy and disorganized, with one teacher and an assistant. All grades had class in the same room at the same time. I had the same teacher from kindergarten through the 9th grade, until the parents pressured the colony leader to get him fired. After 20 years they finally discovered the obvious: he wasn't teaching us what was necessary. I felt cheated to lose all those vital years of learning.

My friend and I decided to continue to 12th grade, and we were ridiculed and mocked by colony members. We heard, "They just don't want to do colony work," and "They are lazy and that's why they're continuing school." At age 15 one is considered an adult and required to work full time for the colony. The only glimmer of hope I had was that my friend and I were in this together. The changes that came to our school were almost overwhelming. Most of our classes were now over the phone. It was the first day of school, with a new teacher and a whole new setup. I was a tall teenager, stuck to my desk, ashamed that somebody might see how much anxiety I had. Anxious, because I quickly realized that I hadn't learned much the previous years and felt incapable of accomplishing what was set before me. It was as if I had just finished 5th grade and now had skipped to the 10th grade.

Was this lack of proper education meant to cure our desire to learn so the colony would reap the benefit of our strong youthful years for free labor? I did not choose my education to be this way. My only other alternative was dropping out. If I dropped out I would never face my fears. The colony leaders would have preferred this and I was becoming a perfect candidate to be a good "slave" that would never leave the colony, the "ark." After all, what kind of education did I really need to work in a chicken barn anyway? I did not allow the colony's wishes to win the upper hand. I struggled through and eventually graduated.

Our school building was old and long overdue for demolition. Just before seeding, the colony invested in a brand new tractor worth several hundred thousand dollars. It was a warm spring day and all the kids in school were excited to see the new tractor drive past the houses to its parking spot. The children crowded around the window. The English schoolteacher was drawn in by the commotion, curious to see what the fuss was all about. After a quick glance she sarcastically remarked, "There goes our school money!"

Shortly after I finished school, that building was condemned by the school division and the colony was forced to supply a new school building. It took someone from the "outside" to recognize that the school was not fit for the children and to demand that suitable changes be made.

My developmental years were used to minimize any potential I would have had for success outside the colony. After high school I was not offered the privilege of an option for higher education. One out of hundreds might be selected to go to a university only when there is a specific need deemed necessary by the colony leaders. The hierarchy control over the colony members was, "Whatever is best for us, is best for you."

One must be married to be elected for most jobs in the colony. The only job available is the one the colony assigns. God gave me gifts and talents for my life, but due to the colony's regulations and demands I was never able to use them. God gave me the talent for mechanical work and welding. Most likely I would have had to work in a chicken barn for the rest of my life.

When I was 20 years old I planned to leave the colony and make a way for myself in the world. I was going to live it up, smoke, drink, party etc. Just a few days before I was going to thrust myself into the world by running away, I sat in our living room around lunchtime listening to my dad talk with a feed salesman. To my surprise God in his wondrous ways intervened and changed my life forever. Out of the blue I heard my dad say something I had never heard from him before. He was joyfully sharing his testimony of receiving Jesus Christ as his Lord and Savior, which had happened just a few days earlier. I didn't know what to think. I was so convicted. I knew I was a sinner and needed to repent and receive Jesus Christ as my personal Lord and Savior. The next four days were the longest four days of my life. In my heart I needed the change that I saw in my dad, yet the ways of the world were incessantly tugging at me. I had it all figured out. I was going to be a self-made man, buy a car, have my own place to live, and be independent. I wanted a woman. I was going to enjoy myself! With everything in me, I fought to justify my selfish desires.

As God would have it, He messed up my plans. Praise the Lord for His grace and mercy! The constant burning of conviction in my spirit drove me to my knees. With all that was in me and with all that I believed I threw myself at the foot of the cross and accepted Jesus Christ to be Lord over my entire life, forever. I noticed an instant change. I had joy. I finally had joy! My old desires quickly vanished, and my heart was swelling with the love of the Lord and my desire to obey Him.

In Luke 15:7 it says, *"I say unto you, that likewise joy shall be in heaven over one sinner that repenteth, more than over ninety and nine just persons, which need no repentance."* The next week my cousin, the colony minister's son, called me and invited me to go to a nearby agricultural show. I told him I was going with my other cousin instead, a cousin who had already been labeled as a "holy roller." With an awkward pause and a quick response the phone call was over. Then I knew our friendship had run its course. It would be assumed that, in a Christian environment when one receives Jesus Christ into their hearts, all others would rejoice with one's confession of faith.

Hutterite leadership does not recognize being born again as an absolute necessity for eternal life. Jesus declared to Nicodemus in John 3:3: *"Verily, verily, I say unto thee, except a man be born again, he cannot see the kingdom of God."* After my dad made a decision to receive Jesus Christ as Lord and Savior, our family was mocked and ridiculed for our faith in the Word of God.

My dad was taken before approximately 30 leaders for questioning. He was asked, "Can you call a Christian from the 'outside' your brother?" He answered, "Yes" and that was the official reason given for my dad being excommunicated from the colony. However in the Word, Jesus said: *"For whosoever shall do the will of my Father which is in heaven, the same is <u>my brother</u>, and sister, and mother."* (Matt. 12:50)

My dad was excommunicated and it was necessary for him to start working outside the colony to earn money so he could get his own vehicle and prepare to leave with his family. I often wondered how he felt, after living most of his life as a Hutterite to suddenly be forced to start from scratch and support his family. The colony refused to give my dad any financial compensation for all his years of hard work and devotion to the colony. We were shunned and mistreated even by our own relatives within the colony. A relative in the colony put a bunch of fence staples in our driveway to flatten our tires, and painted graffiti on our family's vehicles.

When I received Jesus Christ my eyes were opened to see things in the light of God's truth. I instantly had a sincere desire to pray and read the Word of God as much as time would allow. There was a quick realization that I didn't know how to make the Word of God real in my life. My old life of darkness was still tugging at my soul. The Hutterite way of life I had been taught was contrary to the burning desire inside me. God in his loving kindness was using the circumstances in my life to draw me to the truth and to a closer walk with Jesus.

As I look back, I see I had no vision for my life. The Word of God says: *"Where there is no vision, the people perish..."* (Prov. 29:18). I didn't have support from the leaders and other members and even found they were in total opposition to my decision to follow Jesus. I was groping in the dark, looking anywhere and everywhere for godly help... but found none. *"We grope for the wall like the blind, and we grope as if we had no eyes: we stumble at noonday as in the night; we are in desolate places as dead men."* (Isa. 59:10)

Like Jonah in the belly of the fish I was in a place of desperation. It was a place of testing to prove if I was serious about my commitment to Jesus Christ. He was teaching me how to trust and depend on Him to bring me out of the darkness. God blessed me in my decision to finally leave the colony and I haven't looked back since.

Praise be to God!

He heard my cry. *"He brought me up also out of a horrible pit, out of the miry clay, and set my feet upon a rock, and established my goings."* (Psa. 40:2) God showed Himself strong, giving me wisdom and understanding, and by His Spirit brought life to the Scriptures. He gave me true godly leadership which discipled me in the teachings of Jesus Christ in simplicity and truth. I learned to hear His voice and follow Him. Through it all I have a vision and purpose for my life. I trust God to lead me to obey and please Him by His grace and power.

CHAPTER 5

Arise Up Quickly,
And The Chains Fell Off
From His Hands
Acts 12:7

Titus Waldner:
Titus is adventurous and loves the outdoors, animals, and camping. He's a happy person who brings joy to those around him. He is known to his family and friends as "Chuckles" because of his peculiar laugh. Titus is married to his sweetheart, Darlene. Titus is a partner and overseer in a construction business endeavor. He's skilled at interior finish work, drywall and painting, as well as horticulture. Titus is creative in such things as drawing and choreographed praise and worship dance, and plays the drums and harmonica. He is learning to pilot a single engine aircraft. Titus left a colony in North Dakota at the age of 18, a few months after his brother Jason.

I heard the phone ring in the chicken barn. One of the workers called me to the phone. My heart began to pound in anxious anticipation. "Hello," I nervously answered the phone. It was an awkward moment, and yet filled with relief since my hour of decision was at hand.

My brother Jason, who was at our family's home in the colony for a short visit, was on the line: "We're leaving here in a couple of hours. Are you leaving the colony today? Are you coming with us? It's your choice."

It seemed like eternity before I responded with an emphatic,

"Yes!"

Months earlier:

I was riding down a rough winding trail on my bicycle. I rode faster and faster, letting the wind blow on my face. I was miserable, and this was the only way I could briefly escape.

I was 18 at that time, living in a Hutterite colony. I wondered why I was so miserable. I had many questions and was searching for answers. I went for long walks along the river, praying continuously. When I was all by myself in the back of a barn, out of sheer desperation and depression, I couldn't contain the tears and found myself weeping uncontrollably. Nobody could know what I was going through. All those times God heard my prayers. He heard me crying in the barn, and He was the only one that had the answers to all my questions.

"They that sow in tears shall reap in joy." (Psa. 126:5)

What was wrong with me? The problem had to be me. After all, I grew up in a respectable Hutterite family. My father was the colony schoolteacher. He taught me everything he knew of the Bible and the Hutterite way of life. The Hutterites are a direct branch of the Anabaptist faith. Hutterite life itself was supposed to be the best way to live, at least that is what I was told.

It took a long time before I understood that the unreasonable and fanatical religious system in which I was raised was wrong. I had been taught that the Hutterite way of life is superior to every other system. A utopia, if you will, of religious fervency and economic efficiency. What could be wrong with that? It turns out there was much at fault.

Like a tree planted in a very small pot, my roots were just circling around and around the pot until I was choking from lack of air and nutrients. I had been duped to conform to the constricted life of a Hutterite, which caused me to cry out for real peace and freedom.

The Hutterite way of life is extremely regimented, beginning at the age of five and progressively worsening until adulthood. I was hemmed in by the colony's lifestyle and very limited by its restrictive boundaries. One of the first and primary areas of limitation is the Hutterite language. Hutterites speak a secretive dialect, in a divisive tone. Only the Hutterites can interpret it and it isn't written. As a child growing up, the Hutterite dialect was the only language I knew until I began learning English in school at the age of six. I learned to speak some broken English before that, but my only language of influence was the Hutterite dialect. With no chance for any influence other than Hutterite, it's no wonder I was so hopelessly focused on colony life and believed it was the only way of life for me. Why shouldn't I believe what I was told when it was all I ever heard?

It's interesting how the Hutterites cling to their dialect so strongly that it becomes sacred to them. This language thoroughly separated me as a Hutterite child from the rest of the world and would have continued to alienate me in any social interaction for the rest of my life.

As I progressed in school, I learned enough of the English language to begin reading books and soon became a real bookworm. Almost every report card I received had a comment about how I loved books. I know this is one thing God used to help me realize there was more to life than the shadowy little bits and pieces I could experience from colony life. However much the storybooks revealed to me the different world that was out there, those books could not bring me to know how illogical my Hutterite life was. The revelatory Word of God, and understanding the scriptures through teaching, would have shown me the contradiction between real Christianity and the Hutterite form of Christianity. Herein lays a stumbling block: another sacred language. The Hutterite's religious language is High German. The church services, prayers, and songs are all in High German. Strangely enough, it wasn't in the Hutterish dialect that we spoke and understood best. We learned High German, but we never mastered it at all. Even though my dad was the colony German schoolteacher and was immersed in language study, I still did not have enough of a grasp on German to study the Bible in any depth. I can only imagine how much less other Hutterites understand the German language, whose dad is not a German schoolteacher. I was encouraged to read the Bible in German, and so much of what I didn't understand was explained to me according to "the Hutterite interpretation." It was only later that I realized how much I had missed, all the while thinking I was getting everything I would need. Here, again, was a barrier from the truth. I was in the dark and kept from the truth by language, false teachings, and omissions in teaching and training.

The structure of a Hutterite colony causes its members to focus only within the system's narrow confines. They focus best within this religious framework of business and are very uncomfortable outside of it. I remember one project in school where the teacher gave us a whole day to design a floor plan of a house. I revved up my imagination and presented a plan that fulfilled all the dreams I had (the non-Hutterite ones). It had a big swimming pool, a theatre system, and even a small sports arena. My classmate on the other hand, heeding the suggestion of our Hutterite teacher, came up with a house that would fit colony needs. Her cookie cutter house had many rooms, no extravagance, and the least amount of total square footage possible. I couldn't figure out why she did that, but maybe she was just being practical. After all, one couldn't ever build a dream house in the colony, so why bother even thinking about it? Given a few more years of colony life and I would have probably done the same thing. I shudder to think of that now, as I am in leadership in a construction business. God put that creativity in me as a child. If I hadn't obeyed God's calling to leave the colony it would have been bent to conform to the small world within Hutterism, or maybe stifled altogether and would never have been exercised at all!

God has a brighter plan for us, as it says in Jeremiah 29:11: (NKJV) *"For I know the thoughts that I think toward you, says the LORD, thoughts of peace and not of evil, to give you a future and a hope."*

The only future I had in the colony was to give up my own future, my hopes, and my dreams. This wasn't for my spiritual benefit like I was told. All it did was separate me further from God's plan.

The only benefactor was the economic system of the colony. The economy of a colony operates by keeping the members ignorant about the world outside. The majority of financial matters are controlled by the secretary (one of the leaders). The people don't have to worry about taxes, banking, investments, or retirement. All this is taken care of by the colony. Now this may seem pretty good, until you wake up one day and realize you are so dependent on the colony that leaving on your own is a serious risk. If one works for the colony all his life and decides to leave, he risks leaving with no financial compensation. He is at the mercy of the colony's leaders and compensation is minimal, if anything.

Anyone who decides to leave becomes financially stranded with no savings, no investments, and no retirement fund. Also, it is likely they would have little knowledge about economics, from taxes to banking. The control the colony exercises over its people by keeping them dependent is entrapment. This is a big reason why the economy of the Hutterites works so well. As long as economic independence is not allowed for the individual, the colony is assured that few will want to leave.

There will always be those reading this who will wonder, "Is it really that bad?" Yes it is! Is that to say one couldn't have fun in the colony or that there were never any good times? I wasn't particularly unhappy in my early childhood. The fact that I was so dependent on the colony created a false feeling of safety and security, especially when I was younger. I can think back on fond childhood memories, such as playing in the surrounding woods, visiting relatives, and even having fun doing work and chores. I didn't realize how narrow a life I actually had. The things I was being taught as a child were shaping me to become a good Hutterite, and to get me to sell my birthright for the sake of materialistic security.

I was not being trained up to be a good citizen, nor a person of character, nor a good Christian, but instead a good Hutterite. This was evident throughout my upbringing.

For example, I would hear about people who had left the colony and relatives that were living outside, and it was all negative talk. There were many accounts of Hutterites who were "runaways" and were now fully into the sinful world. Another couple had left with good intentions but their children were corrupted because of all the evil influence outside the safety of "the ark."

Wow, I really, really didn't want to end up out there like those poor lost souls. I thought to myself, "If I die like that, I might be in hell." It was simple for me: "Outside English world, bad ... inside Hutterite colony, good." I was taught to assume the devil had everyone on the outside deceived and the colony was the bastion of defense against all that outside evil. Just submit to the colony and its rules and you will be safe from all evil desires, and you've got the best shot at getting into heaven. I was led to believe this, but it is in direct opposition to what the Word of God actually says about the world. The Word of God says in 1 John 2:16-17:

[16] "For all that is in the world, the lust of the flesh, and the lust of the eyes, and the pride of life, is not of the Father, but is of the world."

[17] "And the world passeth away, and the lust thereof: but he that doeth the will of God abideth forever."

We, as humans, are born into this world with a spiritually unregenerated heart. God in His loving mercy and grace extended to man the free will to receive salvation through Jesus Christ, thereby receiving a new heart and the power to overcome the world and all its ways.

The Word of God declares that if one does the will of God he will abide forever. On the other hand, I was led to believe that if I submitted to the will of the leadership of the colony I would abide forever. Hutterites believe they are protected from the effects of the outside world. They believe their system and self-sufficiency will provide the way to heaven. Hutterites say they won't judge the salvation of a non-Hutterite, but they do. In the colony there is a covetous lust for power and position. They zealously conjure a pious, condescending foundational statute, eternally marking anyone who isn't a Hutterite.

Whenever I went outside the colony I would exhibit a separatist attitude. I couldn't help it. After all, I spoke a different language, was dressed in Hutterite clothes, and we would hang together in a pack. In my little mind I was living in the best social, economic, and spiritual system invented on this planet since Bible times. I was taught to think "English people" dressed weird and acted pretty strange. I heard all about it from my peers, my elders, my parents, and the leaders. I simply believed what I was told. They must know better than I. And wouldn't you know, by the age of 12 their conclusions had become my own.

Little by little I was squeezed into a mold that would take away my individuality and make me think and operate like everyone else around me. The constant pressure of having to act according to their inhibiting culture wore on me daily. It steadily worsened, mentally and spiritually. At the age of 15 the physical work load grew worse also. There were many times of physical exhaustion from lack of sleep during the long hours of seeding and harvesting. I remember times when I would park my truck in position to unload and fall asleep instantly as soon as I pressed the parking brake. Someone had to come and wake me so I would back up and unload. I would also fall asleep driving a tractor in the fields, veering off the corn rows, thankfully without ever having an accident. By itself the hard work might have been bearable, but it was combined with a lack of love and a hopeless reality that the oppressive conditions would never change. All I had to look forward to was more of the same. Worse yet, there was no one I could open up to and share my feelings with, nobody that would understand or help me. I was left alone, starving for love. This is what drove me to such a depressed state of mind at age 17 and 18. I was longing for any care or concern for my state of depression. Looking back I realize many around me suffered from this same depression, and we could not find help from within the colony. The only solution offered to me was to continue to serve the colony with all my efforts and trust that everything would finally be resolved. The spiritual emptiness inside me was never resolved. The rituals of Hutterite religion offered a soulish, superficial remedy without clarity of vision or direction.

Is this what drives the alcohol addiction that is so widespread among the Hutterites? The leaders not only allow alcohol, they promote this addiction. It is one of the leaders' responsibilities to supply the alcohol for the colony. My brother and I were asked by the leader in charge to serve alcohol at a wedding to adults and minors alike without distinction. We declined to do it and watched as round after round was offered and served to all, including the young people. This is all too common at Hutterite gatherings. Publicly and privately, alcohol flows freely. The leaders themselves are given over to alcohol in many cases. In the midst of the depression and hopelessness around me, the bold-faced temptation of alcohol could have ruined me. Praise be to the Lord, He kept me from this hellish pitfall many Hutterites fall into. I remained empty and without hope. All I could do was look down and keep stomping the clay and straw to make bricks, just as the Hebrews did in Egypt for many years.

Hutterite doctrine has a particular word for what they hold in highest regard as the goal for proper living: "Gelassenheit." To a Hutterite, it means a total submission of mind and will in a state of tranquility and serenity no matter what happens. I know this goal is never attained by anyone and yet, it has a very powerful influence. In the colony no one's preferences, desires, or goals are intended to mean anything. I always wanted to be an airplane pilot. I might as well have wanted to be an elephant. But, elephants don't fly either! It didn't matter what I desired, even if that desire might have been planted in my heart by God. As a Hutterite, I was never encouraged to find out what God's plan was for my life. It was already chosen for me. I was born a Hutterite and I should stay a Hutterite for the rest of my life, and learn to submit to whatever career the leaders had planned for me. I assumed that was God's plan for me. No one asked, "What do you want to do when you grow up?" It really didn't matter what talents I had. I hardly knew there was such a thing as specific giftings and callings of God.

The Word of God speaks clearly about the gifts of the Father*, and the gifts of the Son*, and the gifts of the Holy Spirit*. I wasn't taught any of this because the Hutterites don't understand, believe, or operate in the practice of most of these gifts. The body of Christ functions in love and unity only when individuals led by the Holy Spirit are trained to know and exercise their giftings and calling. The body of Christ cannot walk in the measure of the fullness of Jesus Christ when these giftings and callings are prohibited or willfully neglected.

"Having then gifts differing according to the grace that is given to us, whether prophecy, let us prophesy according to the proportion of faith..." (Rom. 12:6)

"Having then gifts differing..." but the same Lord working in all. One might think the Hutterites would want this truth since they claim to be all about unity and community. On the contrary, the Hutterite system of today is all about control and keeping people together through fear. My mother told us that when she was a teenager, she and other young people received the gift of the Holy Spirit and prayed with tongues, as spoken of in Acts 2. And because of practicing this gift from God, they were called before a gathering of Hutterite elders and were forbidden to

---

* Gifts of the Father: Rom. 12:3-8   Gifts of the Son: Eph. 4:8-11   Gifts of the Holy Spirit: 1. Cor. 12:4-11

continue to pray in tongues. My mom and others had to promise never to exercise this gift of grace from God. The elders must not have read 1 Corinthians 14:39: *"Wherefore, brethren, covet to prophesy, and forbid not to speak with tongues."*

One cannot be a follower of Jesus Christ without following His commandments. Could Hutterites answer the question Peter and the disciples were asked: *"What shall we do [to be saved]?"* (Acts 2:37) Hutterites don't evangelize and most could not confidently declare they are saved, born again. Interestingly only a few verses later, Acts 2:45 is the verse on which the Hutterites base their whole way of life. Only specific portions of the Word of God are taught to reinforce their twisting of the scriptures and to satisfy their need to further their own objectives. Isaiah's heart was pierced through because of *"...the spoiling of the daughter of my people."* (Isa. 22:4) I am angry with a righteous anger, a pure godly anger. The ministers are the very ones who were entrusted to teach me The Way, The Truth, and The Life. I trusted them with my life, my spiritual life. I trusted them with everything. Instead, the ministers rejected the truth of the pure Word of God. The lies they chose to believe were preached from the pulpit into the hearts and minds of the innocent.

"Do they provoke me to anger? saith the LORD..." (Jer. 7:19)

"Therefore thus saith the Lord GOD; Behold, mine anger and my fury shall be poured out upon this place, upon man, and upon beast, and upon the trees of the field, and upon the fruit of the ground; and it shall burn, and shall not be quenched." (Jer. 7:20)

The Lord God Almighty is furiously angry. I am agreeing with the burden of the Lord's heart. Every passing day the innocent unsuspecting masses are spiritually starving without The Bread of Life and thirsting for The Living Water. The minister's false teachings cause the vulnerable people to exist and feed solely on their heretical teachings. The word heresy means to choose. The dominant use of it in the New Testament is to signify sects, substituting self-willed opinions for submission to the truth, and people who profess opinions independent of the truth (heretics).

The Hutterite sermons never taught me how to receive salvation according to Romans 10:9-10: *[9] "That if thou shalt confess with thy mouth the Lord Jesus, and shalt believe in thine heart that God hath raised him from the dead, thou shalt be saved." [10] "For with the heart man believeth unto righteousness; and with the mouth confession is made unto salvation."*

My fervent effectual prayer is that the gospel of Jesus Christ will be preached in love with all boldness in the power and demonstration of the Holy Spirit. I thank God I was blessed to receive biblical teachings from sources outside the colony, where I learned that salvation is a gift of God only through Jesus Christ. I repented of my sins, believed in my heart and confessed with my mouth Jesus Christ as my Lord and Savior. I accepted His loving sacrifice for my sins and received eternal life through Jesus Christ. These messages of salvation from outside the colony brought a freedom and liberty that mere words could not suffice to describe.

After I received Jesus Christ I assumed I could freely serve the Lord within the colony. As a Christian I was trying to serve and obey Jesus, but the more I tried the more troubled I became. As a Hutterite, I was serving the colony.

I worked for the colony. I made money for the colony. I obeyed the leaders and required their permission

82

to leave for business in town or short visits to other colonies. This is the best it would get for the rest of my life.

By this time I was reading the Word of God in English. I was searching for answers everywhere I thought I would find them. It became obvious that the things Jesus wanted for my life would never be allowed in the colony, and that those in power among the Hutterites had an aversion to me speaking openly about Jesus Christ. *"And they called them, and commanded them not to speak at all nor teach in the name of Jesus."* (Acts 4:18)

What I heard from the leaders in my colony and other colonies as well was totally negative towards being saved, born again. This negativity towards my personal testimony of being saved proved they were against the Word of God. If we are not for the truth of the gospel by faith, then we are against it.

I was desperately searching for an opportunity to break free and leave my tormented life behind. That misery had brought me to my end in a frantic search for truth.

I wanted to leave so badly, but all I had been trained to focus on was to be a committed Hutterite and to live within the colony. The colony mold had hardened around me like a thick shell. I knew if I left to follow Jesus, I would never return to the colony. Just then the phone rang, and I knew I would be committing to a decision of all decisions. It had been easy to imagine leaving, but I never expected it to happen so quickly. Suddenly I was struck with fear of the unknown, but I knew what was right, and that it was God calling me to leave.

My heart was fixed. I made my choice to quickly pack a few belongings and say goodbye to my family. I received no support from my family or the few friends in whom I had confided. Stepping into my brother's car I made a decision that would change my life forever. As the miles began to click away there was a tense gnawing in my belly, but as we drove on the nervous fear slowly gave way to the most satisfying peace I had ever felt. With joy and relief I knew I would never go back.

Through divine intervention Jesus had set me free. My new life in Jesus Christ had just begun. I started to receive the loving help and counsel I so desperately needed. My life now had a purpose in Christ Jesus, to serve Him by helping others. Only a few months after leaving the colony my brother and I helped a teenage girl leave her colony in Canada. She was of legal age and asked for our help to leave. We agreed to assist her, but when she told her parents she was leaving they forbade her to go. In a fit of rage her dad yelled at my brother and me and threatened to get a gun if we helped his daughter escape. He reached into the car, trying to take the car keys while he continued to rant and rave. He followed behind us with his vehicle until we were a good distance away from the colony.

The girl's parents watched her closely so she wouldn't leave her room. Just before they took away her cell phone, she managed to contact us and arrange a place outside the colony grounds where we could pick her up at night. She snuck out her window and walked in the dark to our car, to freedom. The strong wind was blowing across the hardened snow-packed drifts. I vividly remember seeing her walk out of the dark night to our car. She wasn't wearing her Hutterite head covering and her hair was disheveled. There was a mixture of determination and fear on her face. She was sure her relatives were coming after her. She dove into the back seat, gasping for air, insisting that we hurry and leave. As we quickly sped away I soon saw the fear give way to relief. I finally saw the joy and excitement I had experienced after I left mirrored on her face.

Even then my heart's desire was to reach into every Hutterite colony and pluck out every man, woman, and child and bring them to a place of safety. Praise the Lord His *"...hand is not shortened, that it cannot save; neither his ear heavy, that it cannot hear."* (Isa. 59:1)

I thank Jesus Christ for saving me and bringing me out of the colony. I will continue to testify of His greatness and how He will deliver those who put their trust in Him.

Thank You, Jesus.

Then & Now

1st Row: **Jason, Titus**

2nd Row: **Karen, Glenda**

3rd Row: **Darlene, Sheryl**

4th Row: **Rodney, Junia**

and   **Cindy**

Praise & Worship Dance Troupe

"His banner over me was love" Sng. 2:4

And they shall be mine, saith the LORD of hosts, in that day when I make up my jewels...

Mal 3:17

Vacationing in Arizona, Oregon,
Montana, California, and Florida

God's Abundant
Blessings!

CHAPTER 6

She's The Minister's Daughter

Glenda Maendel:
Glenda was born in North Dakota and lived in a Hutterite
Colony for 25 years until she left in 2006. She is the only
one in her family that has left the Hutterite colony. Her
parents were born and raised as Hutterites and Glenda was
also a baptized member of the Hutterite Church. She left the
colony to learn to hear God's voice and follow Jesus Christ.
While being discipled Glenda experienced great joy,
freedom, and welcome changes despite much opposition
from her family. To the glory of God, she persevered and
now walks in the blessings of the Lord. Glenda's marriage
brings great joy to her life and she enjoys ministering
together with her husband who is a minister of the Gospel
of Jesus Christ. She is a secretary and bookkeeper for a
construction company and deeply involved as an
administrator in the ministry. Glenda loves playing the
harmonica, quilting, landscaping, and outdoor activities
such as swimming and physical exercise.

It was an awkward moment. I was anxious to tell my
dad what was in my heart. I knew it was the right time to
tell him, "I am leaving the colony for good." Why was it so
difficult for me to tell him what I knew the Lord was telling
me to do? I knew he would be disappointed and his beliefs
would be challenged. He would see it as all the years of his
effort and dedication being lost to the sinful ways of the
world.

My dad is the minister of the Hutterite colony where I lived with my family for 25 years.

In his mind I was breaking a sacred Hutterite covenant. This is a covenant made during the solemn baptismal ceremony. According to the Hutterite leaders' teachings, before one is to be baptized one must vow before the church to be fully submitted to the church's doctrine and customs. In their way of thinking, the ones being baptized would be proving their faithful allegiance to God. Being faithful is defined as: never leaving the colony.

I grew up believing the Hutterite way of life was the best and only way to live and I didn't want to live any other way. I did my best to be a dedicated Hutterite.

My vision was to have a boyfriend, get married, have children and continue the Hutterite way of life. I was doing everything I could as a good Hutterite woman and understood I was there to generate more money for the colony. I trained myself to think the best of every situation. I didn't like it when people left the colony or talked badly about the system. But, I knew in my heart things were not right. I knew there was more to life than what could be offered to me as a Hutterite.

I used to drink alcohol as a teenager because it was readily available and because of peer pressure. I liked to drink because it made me uninhibited, and I got attention from the guys. When I went to weddings in other colonies I was offered alcohol at the age of 15 and 16. Alcohol was served and supplied in abundance by the Hutterite Church. The farm boss in the colony is put in charge of serving alcohol at weddings. As a minister's daughter I drank more than my fair share. Nobody ever tried to stop me from drinking alcohol or warned me of the dangers. Now that I have received Jesus I see the ugliness of the effects of alcohol.

Around the age of 20, I was visiting a Hutterite colony in Manitoba, hanging out with some single Hutterite men. They were talking filthy, listening to horrible music, and drinking. I knew it wasn't right. I didn't have Jesus in my heart as my Lord and Savior; therefore I realized I was no different than them. After I went home I tried to make changes in my life. I said a prayer by myself to receive Jesus into my heart. I wanted to believe I was saved but I had no one to confirm or encourage me in my confession of faith. While I was in the colony I was never absolutely sure I received Jesus Christ into my heart as my Lord and Savior. Through all those years I was in fearful confusion because of the strange doctrines that were ever before me. It seemed impossible to grasp how simple it is to believe the Word of God and receive salvation through Jesus Christ. As a Hutterite, no one ever asked me if I had received Jesus into my heart or offered to say a prayer with me. Most Hutterites believe that when they get baptized into the Hutterite church they become Christians.

There came a point in my life where I knew in my heart many of the things the Hutterites said and did were not righteous, and I could no longer agree with their teachings. I didn't know what else to do at the time so I attempted to put my differences aside and continue to be a good Hutterite.

There was always a "thing" about pleasing people. One way I tried to please people was going to church every day. I hated going to church because I never fully understood the sermons in the German language. I was so frustrated and bored, my thoughts would go crazy to the point I couldn't control them. I loved it when I had any excuse to miss church. When the church sermons were in English, which was uncommon, it was easier to understand and stay focused.

There were many traditions with which I struggled. If I didn't obey these certain rules, I felt condemned. I was driven to attend breakfast at the colony's dining hall every morning, which was a mandatory routine, and I could not miss any colony work. I learned to do what I was told, just to please people and have a good reputation as a Hutterite. I knew by going to church and to breakfast every day, and never missing any work, I would be accepted as a Christian by leadership in the colony and my peers. Now I realize that becoming a Christian is receiving Jesus into your heart, hearing His voice, and doing what He tells you to do.

[1] *"And it shall come to pass, if thou shalt hearken diligently unto the voice of the LORD thy God, to observe and to do all his commandments which I command thee this day, that the LORD thy God will set thee on high above all nations of the earth:"*

[2] *"And all these blessings shall come on thee, and overtake thee, if thou shalt hearken unto the voice of the LORD thy God."* (Deut. 28:1-2)

Man-made traditions and ritualism cannot bring one into a right standing before God. A change of heart through Jesus Christ and one's obedience in one's walk of faith are the real signs of a true relationship with God.

One morning the women got up early to pick peas, which was a big job for us in the colony. I took more than the recommended amount of Midol pills to ease my pain from cramps so I wouldn't miss picking peas. The women would talk amongst themselves when someone missed work due to being sick. They would wonder if the sickness was really that bad, or if it was just an excuse, maybe too lazy. I was even afraid of going to the doctor or dentist. My fear was of what people would say if I missed any work. There were times when I was sick in the morning and was forced to miss work, but felt better in the afternoon. I wanted to go

94

outside for a walk and some fresh air, but I was so afraid of what people would think or say.

Now, much to my embarrassment, I realize I had those same ugly thoughts towards people who missed work for whatever reasons. Instead of going to the person who was sick, out of concern, and asking how she was doing or what was wrong, I would backbite and speak against her. I grew up in such a critical environment where people talk against each other, gossip and jealously compete, I learned to do it also, even though I knew it was wrong.

When my brother was in intensive care at a Minneapolis hospital because of severe burns he had received, I hesitated to go see him because I was afraid to miss any work in the garden. My friend and I went to the garden to do my share of the work, out of fear of what the women might say if I went to see him. You would think somebody would come up and say, "Go see your brother, he is more important than colony work," or, "We will fill in for you." Nobody said anything. Who really cares? Is there any concern? Is everybody just out for himself?

The reason my brother was badly burned is that he and our cousin were burning copper in the middle of the night so no one would see them. They didn't want to get into any trouble for earning the money the copper would bring them. This was one of their only ways to make money for themselves. My brother poured a pail of gas on the fire and the fire came back at him and he was badly burned. Where in the colony were the care, concern, and safety for these young boys? I don't blame the boys; they worked hard for the colony. All young boys have desires of what they want in life and they are deprived of those desires and dreams in the colony. So, you make a little money on the side, and know this: the leaders don't like it when you do.

It's easy for the leaders when they have access to all the money they want, checkbooks and credit cards.

At the age of 15 I began to work in the colony garden, which was hard, hot work, and plenty of long hours. We had a very big garden in the colony. A great portion of the fruits and vegetables were grown for Farmer's Market in Grand Forks. The women had to hoe, plant, and take care of the produce all summer until harvesting time came. Then we had to pick, wash, clean, and package it to be sold at the weekly Farmer's Market. The day before was always stressful, getting everything ready. Saturday morning the garden boss would head to Grand Forks with two girls to sell the produce. This was another hard day's work. We had to unpack everything, carry all the produce to the stand, make sure that the tables were full and that the empty trays went back to the trailer. We constantly had to bag up whatever people chose to buy. You had to be on your toes. Around noon it started slowing down; then we could go look around to see what other people were selling. After all the hard, hot, long, dusty months of work, the garden boss would only give us $2.50 so we could buy a little treat from the other vendors.

One's life as a Hutterite is pre-planned and decided. In the Hutterite colony when one reaches a certain age, there is a water baptism that is a requirement before someone is permitted to be married. At age 21 I took the step to get baptized. This decision was not difficult because I had a boyfriend and I wanted to get married.

According to the Word of God, baptism in the name of our Lord Jesus Christ is an open-show identification with Christ in death, burial, and resurrection. It is the primary acknowledgement that the believer has accepted Jesus as his Lord and Savior. Baptism in and of itself is not a means of forgiveness and salvation. It is an outward sign of an inward change of heart. Oral confession declares, confirms, and seals the belief in the heart of the Christian. As a Hutterite I never said: "I received Jesus in my heart, and now I'm saved and I want to get water baptized."

According to scripture, as soon as you believe on the name of Jesus Christ and receive Him as Lord and Savior, then it is a command to be water baptized. Hutterites have a set time just before Easter when a baptism ceremony will be held. This usually takes place every two years. A Hutterite rule that must be kept before one can be baptized is to be counseled by the elders of the church every Sunday for six weeks, just prior to baptism. Our group of 15, dressed in black, would walk single file, sober-faced, from oldest to youngest to the houses of the five leaders. We would sit bored, listening to them talk for hours without interaction from us. This six-week period is to verify that you are a qualified candidate as a good Hutterite. All of this counseling and the solemn baptism ceremony could not prove out my salvation in Jesus Christ.

As I prepared to be baptized, much pressure was on me to memorize very long verses in German. These verses were not scriptures from the Word of God. Is this a traditional religious "Hutterite baptism"? Yes it is, but it is not baptism according to the Word of God. Why don't all those baptized as Hutterites stand up and say they are born again and boldly share their testimony? Because most have no testimony of the saved, born again nature. The majority of young people have their eyes upon marriage and know they must first be baptized.

Hutterites believe that if women have their hair parted in the middle it is an outward sign of humility. When I was getting baptized I chose not to have my hair parted down the middle. One of the girls I was being baptized with accused me of being disrespectful. She said this because there was a group of elders from a strict Hutterite colony counseling us, and we were supposed to present a good show of humility.

"Do not let your adornment be merely outward arranging the hair, wearing gold or putting on fine apparel – rather let it be the hidden person of the heart, with the incorruptible beauty of a gentle and quiet spirit, which is very precious in the sight of God." (1 Pet. 3: 3-4) (NKJV)

"...for man looks at the outward appearance, but the Lord looks at the heart." (1 Sam. 16:7) (NKJV)

One can dress as modestly as one wants, but if one's heart isn't right, what fruit will that produce for the kingdom of God?

I was also confronted by the Hutterite elders for talking on the phone with my boyfriend. It was not proper to have any association with my boyfriend during the six-week period before baptism. I was not allowed to see him or even talk to him so I could stay focused on my baptism. Traditional Hutterite baptism is a wearisome task of outwardly proving one's solemn devotion to the Hutterite Church. On the other hand, biblical baptism is a joyous time that you share with everyone, proclaiming salvation and the new life in Jesus Christ.

Hutterite baptism didn't bring me any peace. For years I struggled with overwhelming guilt and condemnation. I was depressed and very miserable. I was under such undue pressure to perform and keep the ceremonial laws, and was afraid of doing something wrong. I wanted to follow the Lord but didn't know how, and the biblical solutions seemed unattainable. I would go for walks down to the river, sitting, praying, and crying for hours to receive direction and answers from the Lord. With no one teaching me how to consistently and clearly hear God's voice, how could I have known for sure what God was saying to me? I got together with Christians in the colony for help, but it didn't get better. When I look back, I realize we as Christians in the colony weren't discipled and therefore, how could we help each other or anyone else? I decided to contact non-Hutterite Christian church leaders outside of the colony who I knew loved the Lord. I wrote to David Wilkerson and Robert Thompson, and they wrote back with encouraging counsel for being strengthened in the Lord. I praise God for the encouragement I received from them, which helped me, but only for a short time. For growth in Christ Jesus one needs personal unity with likeminded believers in continual fellowship and accountability. Jesus discipled his followers. Now, God ordains leaders to teach the people the Word of God and train them by example how to walk it out. Discipleship teaches one how to follow Jesus Christ and have an intimate relationship with Him, which the Word of God confirms in John 12:26: *"If any man serve me, let him follow me; and where I am, there shall also my servant be: if any man serve me, him will my Father honour."*

I had a desire for the inner working of the Holy Spirit through baptism of the Holy Spirit as Peter preached in Acts 2:38: *"Repent, and be baptized every one of you in the name of Jesus Christ for the remission of sins, and ye shall receive the gift of the Holy Ghost."* I knew in my heart the only way I could ever come to the fullness of what God has for me, in service to Him, is by receiving the baptism of the Holy Spirit. It was what God ordained for Jesus, God's only begotten Son. I wanted and needed what God the Father had for me, too. When I was about 23, a few of us young people got together daily, out of a sincere hunger to pray for the baptism of the Holy Spirit. Nothing ever happened because nobody was there to teach and pray for us as Paul did in Acts 19:6: *"And when Paul had laid his hands upon them, the Holy Ghost came on them; and they spake with tongues, and prophesied."*

Praise the Lord, He is faithful and wouldn't leave us without. One day "English" Christians came to visit our colony and shared the Word of God with such clear understanding. They were invited by Jason and Titus' parents, without the leaders' knowledge, to preach and teach. At that time in my life I was so desperate for truth of the Word of God, and hearing about them coming brought much excitement. We were praising the Lord together and having an awesome time. Even though I was with them for only a few hours, I experienced such peace, joy, and freedom in my life. I wanted to learn how to walk in that freedom every day. I remember that I felt in my heart how refreshing it was. After they left I tried to continue in what I experienced because I knew it was real. But just three days later the familiar feeling of shame and condemnation overshadowed me; I was without peace and miserable as ever. "That's it!" I knew I had to have a continual relationship with Jesus Christ with established, likeminded believers who were discipled and firmly built upon the Word of God. I had to leave the colony; I could not live this miserable life anymore. There was more to following the Lord than what was being taught in the colony. The god that I was trained to follow in the colony didn't work for me. This was not Almighty God, the God of Truth spoken of in His Word. I began crying out to the Lord Jesus Christ for direction and answers. What am I supposed to do? Where should I go? The Lord God of heaven and earth clearly spoke to my heart. He gave me scripture confirming in my spirit, commanding me to leave the colony. He opened doors for me, which was totally awesome.

After I left the colony I dedicated my life to the Lord and got baptized in water. I was fully immersed as it says in

100

the Word of God, not sprinkled. My heart was prepared to receive the baptism of the Holy Spirit and I began to speak in tongues. God's grace and blessings brought peace and excitement into my life.

Hutterites believe it is a sin if you get baptized as a Hutterite and then leave the colony. They shun you and say you broke your baptismal vows. Being water baptized in the name of God the Father, the Son, and the Holy Spirit has nothing to do with being baptized into a "church."

"Know ye not, that so many of us as were baptized into Jesus Christ were baptized into his death?" (Rom 6:3)

If I returned to colony life the leaders would demand I once again adopt their frivolous, man-made religious rules. They would demand that I publicly repent before the whole church for leaving the colony; I had broken my baptismal vows and this is considered damnable. Then, I would have to go through punishment for a week or two and would be separated from all the baptized Hutterite members. The separation is a period of shunning where the person being punished is ordered to eat by himself. He must sit alone on the stairs in the entryway of the church. If the person is married he is separated from his spouse for the duration of the punishment, having no contact. Association and speaking with others are limited as much as possible. Only after punishment is one restored as a Hutterite.

The Hutterites believe they are the only people doing the perfect will of God. They say they are "the Ark." Do you remember the story of Noah's Ark? Noah and his family were the only ones saved from the flood. The Hutterites consider the colony a symbol of the ark and only those in the ark will be saved. If you leave the colony you are leaving the Ark. The standard set by the Hutterite leaders is that anyone outside the colony is not a brother or sister in the Lord. Some that choose to say they have brothers or sisters in Jesus Christ outside the colony have caused an uproar with the leaders to the extent of being excommunicated. True believers in Christ Jesus will come from all ends of the earth, not just from the Hutterite colony churches.

[34] "Then Peter opened his mouth, and said, Of a truth I perceive that <u>God is no respecter of persons:</u>"

[35] "But in every nation he that feareth him, and worketh righteousness, is accepted with him." (Acts 10:34-35)

While society makes distinctions among people, God's love and grace are available for all and can be received by whosoever will.

"To the praise of the glory of his grace, wherein he hath made us accepted in the beloved." (Eph. 1:6)

God does not show partiality to anyone. If we walk in righteousness, we are accepted by God. So, how can the Hutterites think they are the only ones doing the right thing? I used to think the same way when I lived in the colony and was taught that people outside the colony were worldly and sinful. I believed it was a sin for women to wear pants, and the Hutterite dress and head covering were the only way a woman could be modest. Now looking back, the way I used to dress as a Hutterite was embarrassing, especially going to town because people would always stare. Hutterites have their own dress code, language, and lifestyle, separating themselves from society.

The question I have for you is: If any individual or group claims to be separated unto God, dresses and speaks so differently, and believes they are the only ones making it to heaven, would you join that group, their belief and lifestyle?

My dad is a leader, an ordained minister in the Hutterite colony. He has been shaped into exactly what the

Hutterite leaders, rules and laws would demand of him. Before a man can become an ordained minister, he must adapt his lifestyle to the "ark" to show himself approved.

I absolutely hated it when the leaders pulled my dad's name out of a hat (literally) to become a Hutterite minister. This form of "casting lots" was not used with any God-given authority after the gift of the Holy Spirit's power was given to the disciples and apostles of Jesus Christ after the day of Pentecost in Acts 2. According to the Word of God, one should be ordained by the Lord and confirmed by men and women of God.

[2] "As they ministered to the Lord, and fasted, the Holy Ghost said, Separate me Barnabas and Saul for the work whereunto I have called them."

[3] "And when they had fasted and prayed, and laid their hands on them, they sent them away."

[4] "So they, being sent forth by the Holy Ghost, departed unto Seleucia; and from thence they sailed to Cyprus." (Acts 13:2-4)

I had a better relationship with my dad before this. He was happier, more outgoing and fun to be around. One thing I really liked was how he would occasionally join in with the young people to play softball or volleyball. I could talk with him freely.

After my dad became a minister he was more serious and strict. Over time I saw him lose his joy and lightheartedness. It was hard for me to talk with him, which caused me to pull away. Even before my dad was minister, my parents and I rarely showed outward love and affection with hugs and "I love you." I couldn't bear to see our relationship get any less. It's not a good feeling as a daughter to be afraid of your dad. I was afraid to share anything personal with either of my parents.

Another reason I hated my dad's minister position was that the people in the colony gossip about and slander the leaders all the time. People slandered my dad right to my face, which hurt, and caused me to become calloused towards him.

Since I have left the colony, I have a love for him I have never had before. I am no longer afraid of my dad. I would do anything to see him set free from the bondage he is under as a Hutterite minister. It hurts to see a man who has such love in his heart for his daughter hide it because of religious beliefs that don't exemplify the heart of God and the actions and words of Jesus Christ. We hardly ever talk on the phone, and I've seen him face to face on the average of once a year. The words are few. The visits are very short, with straight-faced emotions.

While still in the colony I was engaged to be married to someone who had recently left the Hutterites. What did my Dad think about my relationship with the boyfriend I had known for six years? I don't know. We simply never talked about it.

My fiancé and I wanted to get married but received no support because he was in trouble with the Hutterite elders for his bold stand on being born again. He had been excommunicated so there was no option for us to be married in the Hutterite church. He eventually had to leave the colony. I was glad he was leaving his colony because then there might be a possibility of us getting married.

The Hutterite structure of marriage is not established on the foundation of all the truths in the Word of God. We were left to our own ignorance. I was continuously struggling and crying out to the Lord, wondering if this was the man I was supposed to marry. From the beginning of a typical Hutterite couple's dating relationship, there is no vital prayer, communication, godly oversight and counsel from the parents and elders.

Hutterites officially get engaged a week or two before the marriage ceremony in a ridiculous ritual in which the man formally asks the parents for permission to marry their daughter. According to the Word of God the man is to seek permission from the parents at the <u>very</u> <u>beginning</u> of the courtship, not just a week before the wedding.

The Hutterite ritual involves the relatives of the bride and the groom vigorously debating for hours and hours whether or not the couple should be married. This tradition is strictly adhered to and is virtually pointless because permission is always given.

Meanwhile people are in the kitchen preparing food for the engagement celebration. The wedding dresses have already been made and everything is ready for the wedding, which will be held within a few weeks.

During the engagement ritual the only advice given for their marriage stresses the couple's diligent compliance with the Hutterite rules and lifestyle. The colony's demands are placed in priority over the marriage and the family. I certainly wanted to follow the biblical principles of courtship and marriage, but we were provided no opportunity by the Hutterites for the teaching and guidance which couples need throughout their lives.

After I left the colony I finally received teaching according to the Word of God about hearing the Lord's voice. With much prayer and revelation I clearly heard from the Lord that it wasn't His will for my fiancé and I to get married.

How simple it is to hear God's voice and know what His perfect will is. *"For God is not the author of confusion,..."* (1 Cor. 14:33). I experienced life in the colony with only traditions and man-made ordinances to guide me.

Little did I know God had <u>His choice</u> in a man He ordained for me to marry. What a freedom and joy in Christ Jesus to finally know the Lord's heart. He was an "English man," a minister of the Word of God. This time I had the opportunity to be obedient according to the Word of God as led by the revelation of the Holy Spirit.

I made a phone call to tell my parents I was coming to their home to get the last of my personal belongings that were stored there. While I was there I tried to get my parents together to tell them about the man I was to marry. My desire was to arrange a meeting with the four of us so we could ask for their blessing to get married. I called my dad, who was working in the butcher shop. He refused to come to the house and talk face to face with my mother and me. I begged, but he adamantly refused.

I was finally forced to just leave without any resolution. I wrote a letter to my parents asking them to please call me because I had something very important to share with them. Weeks passed and they never responded.

Therefore, I got married without them knowing or caring enough to know. Through it all, we have the Lord's blessing on our marriage and that's what really matters. Had I stayed in the colony, married a Hutterite, and done it the unbiblical, traditional way, my parents would have supported my marriage. Now, I was doing it according to the Lord's way, and I was being ostracized. Why?

In my dad's opinion I was a covenant breaker, a prodigal daughter, and worse yet, if he had known, I married a non-Hutterite. Because of the Hutterites' unbiblical belief, they will not approve or bless Hutterites marrying outside of the Hutterite faith. If you are a Hutterite and leave the colony to marry someone on the outside, that is sin to them. It does not matter if the spouse on the outside is a Christian.

After my parents found out I was married and who he was, they rejected both of us, and our marriage. What hindered my parents from agreeing with my marriage was not only that my husband was an outsider, but the fact that he had been previously married and divorced.

Contrary to scripture, Hutterites maintain a legalistic position that if one remarries while the other spouse is still alive it is always adultery.

In the Hutterite way of thinking there is no exception, although Jesus taught on divorce in Matthew 19:7-9 and said: *"except for fornication."*

In 1 Corinthians 7 Paul clearly distinguished between believers and unbelievers in the standard of accountability on the issue of marriage and divorce. In verse 15: *"But if the unbelieving depart, let him depart. A brother or a sister is not under bondage in such cases: but God hath called us to peace."* When an unbeliever initiates divorce without the believing spouse agreeing, the believer is no longer in bondage to that relationship.

When Jesus talked with the Samaritan woman in John 4, He stated that she had five husbands. Jesus acknowledged all five marriage covenants, because, as Paul wrote, there was a different standard of accountability because she was unsaved at the time.

My parents wrongly judged my marriage without caring to talk with me and without spiritual understanding of the Word of God. They cared more about what people would think and their reputation than the well-being of their daughter and her faithfulness to the Word of God.

My husband called and tried to speak to my dad and meet with him. My dad told him, "No, you're a sinner" and angrily hung up the phone. What kind of parent would not want to talk with his daughter's husband? And this from a "Christian" colony minister!?

Recently, I was involved in a serious car accident and ended up in the emergency room. My husband called my dad once again to reach out and establish a relationship, assuming he would want to know that his daughter had been in a dangerous accident. My husband identified himself by name and immediately my dad angrily responded, "I'm not interested," and once again hung up the phone.

How could a father reject his own daughter?

I have called repeatedly for over four years to get my dad, mom, my husband and me together. They have refused reconciliation on every possible level. My husband is still waiting to see my relationship with them in Jesus Christ made whole. If people have never received the love of God in truth, it is very possible they would not recognize it when it is right in front of them. God forbid that anyone would allow fears or doubts to overtake his conscience.

As a Hutterite I was never taught to be a real Christian. Since leaving the colony, I have been taught through biblically based discipleship what it means to be a true believer in Christ Jesus, and how to walk and live as one.

I find so much more freedom, joy, and peace in loving people and treating them with respect, as the Word of God commands. There are enough people in the world who have hatred towards one another. Where is the love from the people who call themselves Christians?

"Let all bitterness, wrath, anger, clamor and evil speaking be put away from you with all malice. And be kind to one another, tenderhearted, forgiving one another, even as God in Christ forgave you." (Eph. 4:31-32)

"Love suffers long and is kind, love does not envy, love does not parade itself, is not puffed up; does not

behave rudely, does not seek its own, is not provoked, thinks no evil; does not rejoice in iniquity, but rejoices in the truth; bears all things, believes all things, hopes all things, endures all things, Love never fails..." (1 Cor. 13:4-8) (NKJV)

While I was living in the Hutterite colony I thought it was the only place where I was safe and secure. When I left the colony to go to town, I couldn't wait to get back home. Now I realize any place is a safe place, in Jesus Christ. There are many scriptures in the Word of God declaring: God is our refuge. I never once read in the scriptures that "the colony" would or could be my refuge.

"...my refuge is in God." (Psa. 62:7)

"...God is a refuge for us." (Psa. 62:8)

In the colony I never knew God as my refuge or someone I could trust. I was in constant fear, especially going for walks by myself. I never knew I could trust God to care for me, provide for and watch over me, and protect me from evil. I wish I had been taught these truths, because I lost those years to unnecessary fears.

"The fear of man brings a snare, but whoever trusts in the Lord shall be safe." (Prov. 29:25)

I thank the Lord God for what He brought me out of and where I am now. I have learned to hear His voice, walk in the Spirit of God, and be obedient to what He commands me to do. I now have the power and strength to fulfill His heart's desire for me.

I have been taught about God's heart and ways since I've left the colony. I am being discipled; I have received deliverance and healings, and experienced miracles, signs and wonders. I could go on and on forever, all to the glory of Almighty God! There is no turning back. I will never give up following the Lord Jesus Christ and everything I have in Him. I have been and am continuing to be truly blessed. <u>God's desire for everyone, everywhere, even to the end of days, is to come to the fullness of what He has for them.</u>

"He hath shewed thee, O man, what is good; and what doth the LORD require of thee, but to do justly, and to love mercy, and to walk humbly with thy God?" (Mic. 6:8)

Bless the name of the Lord, Jesus Christ!

CHAPTER 7

"Here Am I; Send Me."

Just days before I left the colony I experienced the
presence of the Lord and knew how wretched and
miserable I was. I knew in my heart the Lord was calling
me. *"Then said I... send me." (Isa. 6:8)*

Cindy Waldner:
*Cindy is friendly, diligent, and outgoing. She is enterprising
and owns her own cleaning business. She's debt free and
trusts in the Lord for His provision with a childlike faith.
Cindy loves to play the piano and listen to classical music.
She is a talented seamstress: she designs and sews flags and
dance clothing for a Christian dance troupe. Her prayer life
in ministry is a vital part of her walk with her Lord and
Savior Jesus Christ. Cindy is observant and sensitive with a
heart to serve the needs of others. She is an older sister to
Junia and Karen who are all now citizens of the United
States.*

I remember sitting in my room as a young Hutterite
woman, 23 years old, praying to the Lord:
"What is my future, Lord, what is your plan for my
life?" I could see my life spread out before me and saw
nothing of a future promise. "After 23 years as a Hutterite,
this is it!?" But I had received the Lord just a few years
before and I remembered the feeling of joy and elation in
my decision to follow Him. Maybe the problem was in my
colony and another colony would be better. I knew for sure

that life had more to offer than what was previously set before me. I couldn't wait anymore.

I mustered up the courage to call my aunt who lived in a different colony to see if I could move in with her family. Her husband was the minister of that colony. They agreed to take me in. After living there for a few months a small ministry from the U.S. was invited by my uncle, the minister, to come and share the Word of God. They were Christians, filled with the Spirit of God, were well grounded and established in the Word of God. As soon as they entered the living room my uncle quickly moved to the large bay window facing the colony kitchen and hastily pulled the curtains shut. He feared what other colony members might say if they found out these "English people" were here to minister the gospel of Jesus Christ. We had fellowship, breaking of bread, and prayer; the minister from the U.S. humbly washed my uncle's feet. One of his daughters, my cousin, received the Lord into her heart that evening. After receiving the Lord she and I received the baptism in the Holy Spirit and spoke in tongues.

At the end of the meeting my uncle approached the leader of the visiting ministry and thanked him for coming and ministering to his family. He went on to boldly say, "Nobody can tell me this meeting wasn't of the Lord, this was of the Lord!"

A few from the ministry were invited to spend the night. The next day there were hearts turned to the Lord, and water baptisms.

My eyes were opened and I saw everything in a new way. I went to the community kitchen and church services and I knew my days as a Hutterite were numbered. Within a couple of days I was so stirred in my spirit, I became restless. I realized I couldn't ever fit into the dead structure of the Hutterite order. I earnestly prayed a bold, desperate prayer asking my Father in Heaven to help me and lead me in the way of truth. And He, being ever true to His Word, spoke to my heart and confirmed it with scripture. At that moment He gave me a very clear vision to leave the Hutterite colony and go to the United States, to be ministered to and discipled by the ministry that had come to preach the Word of God.

Now I understand that at that moment God testing my faith by not allowing me to go to the States right away. I was not accustomed to waiting upon the Lord in faith and this made me very uncomfortable. I praise the Lord I had no other place to go since I chose to follow Jesus with all my heart. I had moved to the colony I thought to be the best option available to me, and suddenly understood this colony was no better than the one I had left. It was the Hutterite system that had been the problem all along. I was learning to trust God and I knew His eye was upon me.

I was encouraged because God showed me the problem and the way out through the vision He had given me to leave the colony. He confirmed it with this scripture:

[17] "Wherefore come out from among them, and be ye separate, saith the Lord, and touch not the unclean thing; and I will receive you,"

[18] "And will be a Father unto you, and ye shall be my sons and daughters, saith the Lord Almighty." (2 Cor. 6:17-18)

By remaining in the Hutterite system I would have compromised my faith in Jesus Christ. I obeyed the inner promptings of the Holy Spirit to leave for good. With determination I called my dad, who had recently left the Hutterite Church, to come and get me at my uncle's house and take me to the ministry in the U.S. My dad agreed and I enthusiastically packed my bags and was ready to go when he showed up. As we drove away there was only joy and great expectation of a whole new life in front of me.

We are created in the image of God; we should never be pleased to dwell on a level of existence lower than what God has purposed for us. We are accountable and responsible to God to walk in the ability and capacity we have been given as human beings. We must strive to be all God has called us to be to reach the highest standard possible. To do any less is to be unfaithful stewards of the life God entrusted to us. God's ultimate plan for humanity is ideal, in the sense that each individual possesses gifts and talents that differ one from another, so the human race can be furnished with all its needs met.

As a Hutterite, one of the things I struggled with the most was not knowing that God had a plan and purpose for my life. God created me as an individual to be a shining example as a servant, to worship and glorify the Lord Jesus Christ! The Word of God declares:

[1] *"Praise ye the LORD. Praise God in his sanctuary: praise him in the firmament of his power."*

[2] *"Praise him for his mighty acts: praise him according to his excellent greatness."*

[3] *"Praise him with the sound of the trumpet: praise him with the psaltery and harp."*

[4] *"Praise him with the timbrel and dance: praise him with stringed instruments and organs."*

[5] *"Praise him upon the loud cymbals: praise him upon the high sounding cymbals."*

[6] *"Let every thing that hath breath praise the LORD. Praise ye the LORD."* (Psa. 150:1-6)

As a little girl I had a burning desire for music and playing the piano. My younger sister and I would go into the attic of our home and record ourselves singing while I played my little red toy piano. It was planted into my heart by God, but I was taught to think it was not fitting for women to play a musical instrument or to express in dance the freedom and liberty of our heart's desire. I couldn't imagine singing an English song or anything other than a German religious hymn in the Hutterite church. As a rule, in the Hutterite colonies musical instruments are not fitting nor allowed in church services, and few exist for personal use. Praise the Lord, I have my own piano. It is such a blessing and freedom to fulfill the command of our Lord to glorify Him through instruments and vibrant, interpretive dance in the Spirit, which is an outward expression of the life of Jesus that works in me. This truth has set me free! Now, it is a joy unspeakable to know and experience the depth of intimacy that exists between our Lord Jesus Christ, Father God Almighty, and His beloved saints. I could finally be all that God created me to be.

"So God created man in His own image, in the image of God created He him; male and female created He them." (Gen. 1:27)

Every Christian woman is called and commanded by God to boldly teach, prophesy, evangelize, and preach the Word of God as led by the Holy Spirit. They can pursue a career, lead in business, and exercise their spiritual giftings and God-given talents to bring Him glory through a life of freedom. God's expression of love for women is no less than for men. They have equal value in God's eyes and therefore equal access to all the gifts of grace from God. Under God's divine order for protection and blessing, the head of every man is Christ and the head of the woman is the man.

"...the head of every man is Christ; and the head of the woman is the man; and the head of Christ is God." (1 Cor. 11:3)

So, what is expected of a woman in the Hutterite system?

A Hutterite woman is demanded to wear a very specific pattern of dress. These can be made two different ways with only one petty, minute difference, but really, there is no difference (Interestingly I had both patterns, and certainly neither one got me closer to God). She is commanded to wear a black head covering at all times. The men, elders, and others see this embarrassing garb as being modest. She is also required to stay silent and constrained to perform only the things she has learned so well: cook, clean, work in the garden, and make her family's clothes, all of which have the same homely, boring look. Women are strictly forbidden to preach the Word of God and cannot be in any church leadership position. You will find that Hutterite women don't openly confess they have accepted Jesus Christ into their heart as Lord and Savior. Is it perhaps they don't know Jesus as Lord and Savior or are they simply not willing to obey the Word of God?

In most colonies women are not allowed to have a driver's license. I sorrowfully recall the incident when my sister's husband was losing his eyesight, severely restricting his night vision. Out of desperation she obtained her driver's permit without the colony leaders' knowledge so she could secretly drive at night. When the leaders of the colony heard about it they demanded she give up her permit and stop driving. This was all done without compassion and understanding for her and her husband's safety. Keeping their religious man-made rules was more important than someone's life and well-being.

Hutterites cannot be baptized until about 20 years of age. They must go through all the baptismal rituals and cannot share their own personal testimony at the baptismal ceremony. They cannot marry someone who is not a

Hutterite. Men and women alike must be baptized into the Hutterite church or they are not permitted to get married. At age 20 I made the decision to get baptized as a Hutterite. Not once did any of the leaders ask me why I wanted to be baptized; they only questioned if I was too young. I had prayed several months previous to receive Jesus into my heart as my Lord and Savior. I knew just enough that the Word of God commands believers in Jesus Christ to be baptized. I was naïve and never taught the biblical way of baptism and therefore didn't realize I was being baptized into the Hutterite church system with its membership vows and rituals. My personal testimony didn't matter as long as I kept all the traditions and followed all the rules that would qualify me for the Hutterite baptism.

The evening before the baptism it was ultimately demanded for me to go and confess my sins to the minister. I approached the church in the dead of night, opened the door, and entered into the main hallway. Everything was completely dark. I slowly crept in, shuffling my feet in the darkness, and heard a man's deep echoing voice from somewhere in the church. This freaked me out. He ordered me to come sit next to him, but I couldn't see him. I stood frozen for a moment waiting for my eyes to adjust to the darkness, and then proceeded to sit at his side on the church pew. A barrage of questions immediately flew into my mind: Why was I sitting in the dark? Did I want to tell this man anything? This was a leader with whom I had never had a personal conversation! How long was this going to take? After just a moment of telling my typical childhood faults and the teenage sins of watching TV, going to two or three hockey games, and kissing boys, he dropped the bomb. "Did you ever go all the way?" He was my great uncle and this only proved that no relationship had ever been built between us, and therefore he did not know me at all. I was glad to answer "no" and I was immediately dismissed. Only fear surrounded me, certainly not the freedom that comes from confessing one's sins.

The Hutterite elders lack spiritual understanding concerning water baptism according to the Word of God. The Hutterite baptism is driven by fear. I had an overwhelming fear of having to memorize and recite the Hutterite's dead letter of powerless pages of material. I went blank while reciting the assigned poem of 16 rambling verses. God's desire was for me to proclaim the testimony from my heart and not mere memorization from my head. I struggled with having to be baptized by leaders who were unregenerate. At the baptism ceremony the leaders sprinkled a bit of water on my head, which I barely even felt. Now, having come to understand the truth as it is written in God's Word, it is plain and simple to see that full immersion baptism is as God has ordained.

This scripture clearly shows how Jesus was baptized: *"And Jesus, when he was baptized, went up straightway out of the water: and, lo, the heavens were opened unto him, and he saw the Spirit of God descending like a dove, and lighting upon him."* (Matt. 3:16)

Also in Acts 8:38-39 they went down into the water and came up out of the water. This is how God the Father ordained His only Begotten Son Jesus Christ to be baptized. Why should anyone baptize differently? If immersion was good enough for Jesus, it's good enough for me. The meaning of the word "baptize" in the Greek, means to make whelmed (that is, fully wet), cover wholly with a fluid, to dip. Sprinkling is not the way Jesus was baptized and He shall be my only example. Christians who understand the Word of God know that baptism means full immersion. Perhaps these Hutterite ministers haven't had the revelation by the Holy Spirit that Jesus was immersed under His

Father's command. The Hutterite baptism is absolutely and unequivocally not based upon scripture, and is not fit or effective for the kingdom of God.

Since I have left the colony I have experienced a full immersion water baptism that is according to the Word of God. It was a joyous, fearless expression of an inner change of my heart. It's always wisest to rely on the counsel of the truth in the Word of God rather than trust in man's ways in attempting to fulfill God's commands.

My prayer for those who read this book is that they would desire to know Jesus Christ and for their hearts to be open to receive the whole truth. As I sit reading what I have written, I remember the intense longing I had for God's grace and divine revelation that is able to bring deliverance from legalistic bondage. God has now given me the desires of my heart. Hallelujah!

"There is no fear in love; but perfect love casteth out fear: because fear hath torment. He that feareth is not made perfect in love." (1 John 4:18)

When we experience God's love for us and choose to love Him with all of our heart His perfect love casts out all fear. Praise the Lord for His goodness and love!

I am writing this as a message of hope: "Young women, Hutterites, whoever you are, don't permit anyone to shut you down or stop you from fulfilling the divine calling God has on your life. We as Christians are commanded to fearlessly and boldly preach the Word of God. Men and women, take a stand for truth no matter what the cost."

"Preach the word; be instant in season, out of season; reprove, rebuke, exhort with all longsuffering and doctrine." (2 Tim. 4:2)

Recently, a few of my ex-Hutterite cousins and I met several young Hutterite women at a shopping mall. We spoke with them about Jesus and asked if they were

Christians. They said, "Yes" and we asked if they were "born again." They said, "Of course not, we are not of that kind." We told them what the Word of God declares in John 3:3: *"Jesus answered and said unto Him verily, verily, I say unto thee except a man be born again, he cannot see the Kingdom of God."* They replied with an abrupt, defensive, "It does not say that."

It breaks my heart to see these women not being taught the truth of the Word of God. A Christian is a follower of Jesus Christ. The Hutterites claim to be Christians and believe the written Word of God. Why is it, when I was in the Hutterite colony and I prayed the prayer to accept Jesus into my heart as Lord and Savior, I was ridiculed and told I have a false religion? I heard it said that when a baptized member leaves the colony he is damned and going to hell for leaving the Hutterite way of life. Salvation and eternal life come only by the grace of God through faith in Jesus Christ, and not through some religious form of thinking and living.

There was a time, prior to my walking in freedom with the Lord Jesus, when I could not bare my soul and share my innermost feelings and God-ordained desires. The aggravating emptiness and darkness surrounding me held me bound in a dreadful fear.

As a Hutterite teenager, I clearly remember rising from a deep sleep and sensing a spiritual darkness about me, a presence of evil that dominated a specific area of my bedroom for over an hour. Many, many times I was paralyzed with fear; I felt incapacitated to move and had difficulty breathing. Since I left the Hutterite colony's way of life, I have never once had those frightening visitations and experiences of evil walls closing in around me. If only I could have known then what I know now. At the earliest age of accountability, every disciple of Jesus Christ should be taught how to pray, and to understand the profound effect of spiritual warfare prayer and praise. Now that I have been taught to boldly stand against the wiles of Satan and his demons, I am victorious by speaking in the name of Jesus Christ, the Word of God in the power of the Holy Spirit. Through all the years of growing up as a Hutterite it was instilled in me that the colony was a safe place protected from the outside world. I was taught that everything on the outside was evil and in the Hutterite colony we were Christians who loved each other. Why did I not hear about salvation through Jesus Christ until I was around 19 years of age and that from an outside influence? The Word of God says in Rom. 10:9-10: *"That if thou shalt confess with thy mouth the Lord Jesus and believe in thine heart that God hath raised Him from the dead, thou shalt be saved. For with the heart man believeth unto righteousness; and with the mouth confession is made unto salvation."*

At the time I accepted Jesus I started reading an English Bible. It was easier for me to understand than the German Bible, because I barely knew any part of the German language. My eyes were opened and I began to see the hypocrisy all around me. I didn't understand how people could profess to be Christians and say they love God and yet treat one another with an angry disrespect.

I grew up surrounded by hatred, jealousy, strife, bitterness, and unforgiveness, and all the while they covered this with a whitewash, desiring to appear holy. I saw very few loving acts, very little loving emotion or care for one another. Relationships within the colony are shallow even among family members. The harder you work the more you're accepted. When competitive jealousy enters within a closed-society situation, the people involved will turn on one another in critical judgment. Most are suspicious, slanderous, and operate in envious retaliation with a veneer of self-righteous justice.

Long-buried frustrations lead to anger and short outbursts of controlled rage, which lead to sickness: mental, physical, and emotional.

In the Hutterite dialect there is no word for love. When a couple expressed their love for one another they would say, "I love you" in English. The closest word for love in the Hutterite dialect translates to "cute," "like," or "lovely." To say "I love you" from the heart has an entirely different impact than to just say something endearing in Hutterish.

I praise God for loving care and patient discipleship. Through this I have come to know what godly love really is and how it looks and feels, and what it means to lay down our lives for one another. All praise to the Lord Jesus Christ for making a way for me to be taught the character of the Lord Jesus Christ through discipleship! Discipleship is the act of being taught with understanding what the Word of God truly says, and trained in how to walk it out in the Spirit of God, moment by moment, for your whole lifetime.

I am sincerely and deeply concerned for the people who are still continuing in the Hutterite system. We have the right of freedom of religion in the United States and Canada. However, if people are never told the truth how can they choose anything other than what they know? While people are controlled through soulish, emotional ploys they can never be free to live life with the fullness of joy that God promises. When a person chooses to be a Christian and learns to follow and serve the Lord Jesus Christ, then God's promises will be experienced in peace, joy, wisdom, and power.

In the Hutterite colony there is no spiritual understanding to teach men and women the basic spiritual principles concerning the Word of God. I don't remember ever having a spiritual conversation or just a normal everyday conversation with the leaders in the Hutterite colony where I grew up. I had uncles who were ministers and secretaries, and it is saddening to know I never had a conversation of any depth with them. Where were the safety and protection, love and care for me? I was struggling and hurting with issues concerning life. When I was a little girl I was a victim of sexual improprieties, which affected me for years in many areas of my life. I didn't know how to deal with them. As I grew into young adulthood, I learned what had happened to me and finally understood why I often felt as though I wanted to die. I had no one to talk to who could teach me and help me get through the problems I had. There was no discipleship, no spiritual discernment of God, or godly accountability. What a blessing it would have been to hold each other accountable for our actions. Each one is on his own, feebly trying to make it work, but it can't go anywhere. All praise to God for making a way for me to get help when I desperately cried out: "Lord, I need your help; I can't go on living like this any longer!"

Now I have victory, inner peace, confidence, stability, and joy from knowing who I am in Jesus Christ. I am a successful small business owner, I own a car, glorifying God through it all, hearing the voice of God and obeying all He commands me to do. Praise God!

Whoever and wherever you are, if you want all that God has, you don't have to be alone. Call upon the name of the Lord Jesus Christ. He is real and He hears you. He will answer. Seek the Lord Jesus Christ and you will find Him!

CHAPTER 8

No More Rattling Bones

Eze. 37:5 "Thus saith the Lord GOD unto these bones;
Behold, I will cause breath to enter into you,
and ye shall live:"

Darlene Waldner:
Darlene is fun to have around and has a good sense of humor. Darlene has a passion for music and dance. She loves to praise and worship the Lord in dance and is currently taking singing lessons. The music artist that most influenced Darlene to pursue an interest in singing was Barbra Streisand. Darlene has a tender, loving relationship with Father God, and is fully dependent and trusting in Him. She has a keen insight when she prays in communication with God and boldly declares what the Father speaks to her. She left a Hutterite colony in Manitoba, Canada in 2006. Then in 2008, she married Titus and is now a citizen of the United States. She enjoys married life and is a co-owner in a family business. She occasionally helps her husband with his drywall and painting business. The people who know Darlene deeply admire her for her servant's heart and she is dependable, always ready to join in to help. While in the colony, Darlene suffered for several years from a debilitating eating disorder called anorexia nervosa. She found complete deliverance through the power of God in the name of Jesus Christ. She has been built up in Christian discipleship and is trained to help others overcome similar situations.

"No man can serve two masters: for either he will hate the one, and love the other; or else he will hold to the one, and despise the other. Ye cannot serve God and mammon." (Matt. 6:24)

No man can serve two masters; to try to do so is utter misery. I found myself in this situation living in the Hutterite colony. I was ready to turn my heart over to the Lord Jesus and serve Him. There was another master that demanded my service: the colony. I knew I had to make a choice. I started to see that I could not be a good Hutterite and a follower of Jesus Christ.

I began hearing about those who had left the Hutterite faith and a number of young Hutterites who were claiming to be saved, born again. These words stirred my heart and confirmed what I had felt for a long time. I knew there was something more, something different! I began to discover it is possible to have a personal relationship with a lifetime commitment to Jesus Christ, which I had never heard under the colony's teaching. I longed for the void in my heart to be filled. The Lord was drawing me to Himself. I needed godly leadership to teach and train me according to the truth as it is written in Jeremiah 3:15: *"And I will give you pastors according to mine heart, which shall feed you with knowledge and understanding."*

I was duped as a child into believing that serving Jesus and serving the colony are one and the same. What a cunning deception it turned out to be! The love and concern for an individual isn't there. The colony is more about making and hoarding money than providing for the needs of the people. This was especially true for the women's needs. The men had all the expensive equipment. After all, they made the money for the colony. The women slaved away cleaning, gardening, cooking, and raising children, which we all know could only generate a minimal income. So, even necessities were given grudgingly to the women in the colony.

"Every man according as he purposeth in his heart, so let him give; not grudgingly, or of necessity: for God loveth a cheerful giver." (2 Cor. 9:7)

God loves a cheerful heart that gives. I was never taught about giving according to the Word of God. I never experienced God's blessings on my life by being obedient to God's Word concerning giving. Every example of giving I saw was done grudgingly and out of duty.

When I was 11 years old, my dentist told me I needed to have braces. I would hear from the people in the colony how unimportant and expensive braces were. They belittled me and made me feel guilty. When I had an appointment, my dad had to ask for the money to pay the dentist each time. It would have been easier and less painful to have my teeth pulled than ask for the money to have them straightened. Anyone who's ever had braces knows they're painful, inconvenient, and are certainly not for pleasure! I senselessly felt guilty and thought I would be indebted to the colony for the rest of my life. What happened to giving *"to all men, as every man had need"* or having *"all things common"* as the Hutterite's favorite scriptures say in Acts 2:44-45: [44] *"And all that believed were together, and had all things common;"* [45] *"And sold their possessions and goods, and parted them to all men, as every man had need."*

As a Hutterite one cannot own anything, as is clearly written in the Hutterite Constitution, therefore they can't sell *"their possessions and goods"* and give them as they see need. It is true every human has a God-given free will, but in the colony everyone is bound by the Hutterite Constitution from the cradle to the grave.

The Hutterite Constitution Article 40: *"Each and every member of a Colony shall give and devote all his or her time, labour, services, earnings and energies to that Colony, and the purposes for which it is formed, freely, voluntarily and without compensation or reward of any kind whatsoever, other than herein expressed."*

Every person is forced to do everything for the colony. It is wise to not question the reigning authority. Be silent, for you do not have a choice in the matter. One or two of the leaders are in charge of all the money and distribute it as they will. We were told all of our needs would be supplied. What I didn't know was that when I needed something, the authority dictated whether I needed it. The overbearing rule used fear to exercise control over the people's housing, education, work, clothing, health and hygiene.

I was taught that the dress I had to wear was the only way to be modest and perfectly fulfill the Scriptures. I have not found in the Word of God that I need to wear anything of the Hutterite style and colors to be modest. I was taught that the reason the "English people" take a second look at Hutterites is because we are a light to the world with our modest dress and head covering. I knew it was because I stuck out like a sore thumb. I wasn't portraying light to the rest of the world, who have the free will to wear what they choose. It was all a pretense of holiness and modesty. I couldn't witness Jesus Christ to anyone. I had nothing to offer; I myself was lost. All the while I felt deeply wretched inside. Now I have the freedom to dress modestly and be a witness for Jesus Christ without looking odd. It's so much fun to go clothes shopping. I love to look at all the different colors and fashions of clothes. Praise the Lord Jesus! I can buy what looks good on me. It's wonderful to not have just one style or certain color of clothing.

The colony leaders would determine how often I could leave to go to town or visit another colony. I had to tell them where I would be going and get permission from them, knowing they had the power to say no at any time without any rational justification. I recall one instance when my cousin and I went together to request permission from the minister to visit another colony. It might not sound like a big deal, it was just another colony, but we were terrified to approach him. We earnestly prayed beforehand for God's help. You see, some colonies were harder to get permission to visit than others, particularly those with youth that confessed to be born again. I don't know whether to laugh or cry at how extremely small our world was. The established protocol of having to ask for permission to visit wasn't for our protection; their motive was to control the people.

As far back as I can remember my life was controlled by constant fear. For the 20 years of my life in the colony I was motivated by a nagging, tormenting desire to please people. The unhealthy fear caused me to feel empty and unloved and drove me to religiously follow man-made ordinances that were not in agreement with the Word of God. I learned to obey the colony rules and promptly did what I was commanded to do. These regulations produced a slow death in me. I was suffering from depression and had absolutely no hope. I had no way of knowing the joy and peace that comes from following Jesus Christ.

In my mid-teens I began to be plagued with a deadly eating disorder called anorexia. I was overly self-conscious and resorted to extreme measures to religiously punish myself with my erratic eating habits. The only time I didn't feel condemned was when I was fasting; consequently I would starve myself most of the time. The waves of fear were trying to overtake me. This eating disorder could have destroyed my life, had I not left the colony at the time that I did. I felt demonically possessed, like a devil had control of my life. I confined myself to my bedroom and all I could think of was what I would allow myself to eat and how it would taste. In my mind I was a hungry glutton. I was numb, destroying myself and becoming a loner. The crazy side of this was that when I left my bedroom I stepped into another world where I was burning with deep-seated frustrations, progressing into a seething anger. I couldn't wait to get back into the safety and familiarity of my room, where I wasted away year after year.

Proving my self-worth and attempting to measure up to daily expectations were impressed upon me by colony life. I found myself in frantic fear and extreme self-discipline to avoid gaining weight. In my twisted thoughts I was attempting to please God, and all the while I was in total denial that my behavior was abnormal. I knew nothing of God's grace and forgiveness. This life-threatening condition was caused by the ignorance and complete absence of spiritual knowledge and understanding surrounding me. I had entrusted my health and well-being to the adults and others in the colony and none came to my aid. My parents catered to my eating habits in any way they could in order for me to stay alive. I would hear from my cousins how my parents talked about my eating problems behind my back. This separated me from them and made me angry with them, causing me to withdraw even deeper into my dismal state. My family and friends wanted me to eat more; I angrily defended my warped philosophy and state of mind. I was demonically out of control and had become hardened against physical reality and common sense truths. My physical senses were deteriorating. I became obsessive and consumed with cleanliness. I was dangerously germophobic. Everything was dirty, filthy, unhealthy, and detestable to me. I was falling fast and I couldn't stop. I became reclusive, fearing the worst of all things: germs. If I stayed away from everybody I wouldn't be susceptible to "deadly, killer germs," and wouldn't have to cater to the "unreasonable" requests for me to eat. I put my parents through a living hell. I don't blame them; rather I have a deep compassion for them for having to deal with me during this problem. They did the best they could. The colony never prepared my parents to deal with spiritual or physical matters such as addictions and obsessions. I deeply love my parents and hold nothing against them. When I did not understand the root of my problems I had misplaced anger toward my parents. I am truly sorry, and now am righteously angry against the colony system and hold it ultimately responsible.

My dad had been the Sunday schoolteacher for 18 years when he became a believer in Jesus Christ. Yes, he taught us the Bible for 18 years, but he didn't know Jesus as Lord and Savior. My dad had a drinking problem, with outbursts of anger and swearing. In an unexpected yet welcome turn of events, my dad's heart was touched by the convicting power of the Holy Spirit. He received the Lord Jesus into his heart and had obvious changes in his life. All hell broke loose after my dad shared his testimony with the children and young adults in Sunday school. Fearlessly he testified and declared he had lived for the devil and now lives for the Lord. The news spread like wildfire from colony to colony, as if my dad had committed a heinous crime.

During the next few months there was a rumbling of busy chatter that the Hutterite ministers were coming to inquire about the series of events that had taken place, and confront my dad.

On multiple occasions an invasion of over 30 ministers, with matching black coats and hats, systematically entered the church poised to eradicate beliefs that were contrary to their legalistic and pharisaical laws. It was of dire necessity that they judge and pass sentence quickly to stop this preaching in the name of Jesus Christ. This staunch religious procession was motivated by a self-imposed authority which always proves to be false. Shortly thereafter, another invasion converged to further the investigation. My dad's testimony was deemed scandalous by the black coats, a direct violation to their Hutterite code, and led to his being ousted as the Sunday schoolteacher over the young adults and children. The black coat committee pressured the minister of my colony to remove my dad from that noble position. He also lost his job as the German schoolteacher, his manager position over the chickens and turkeys, and his responsibility for the colony's combine.

The ministers strongly insisted my dad compromise and retract his testimony but he boldly stood and refused to deny the Lord who saved him. One of the Hutterite ministers, notable amongst them, was handpicked to confront my dad at my uncle's home, which proved to be a futile attempt to pressure him into submission. My dad stood firm.

[40] "And to him they agreed: and when they had called the apostles, and beaten them, they commanded that they should not speak in the name of Jesus, and let them go."

[41] "And they departed from the presence of the council, rejoicing that they were counted worthy to suffer shame for his name."

[42] "And daily in the temple, and in every house, they ceased not to teach and preach Jesus Christ." (Acts 5:40-42)

After months of meetings the frustrated ministers failed on all counts to convince my dad that the Hutterite way of life and doctrine were the only way to salvation. The committee, reluctant to admit defeat, agreed that my dad should be excommunicated from the Hutterite church. It was one thing to imagine what it would be like to leave and quite another when I saw that final day quickly approaching. When my dad came home and shared the final verdict, it was difficult to fathom that all the leaders had ostracized our family due to our unwavering faith in Jesus Christ. It was very confusing for me because our family scarcely talked about what we were going to do now that my dad was kicked out. He acted like everything was just fine. I can only imagine what he felt when the colony refused to give him any money for all the years he worked for the colony. He was in his mid-40s, with a family, and had to start from nothing to build a new life.

What was I going to do? Could I survive and prosper outside the colony? After all, I knew nothing about how to function in the outside world. I did everything I could to keep my feelings inside. One part of me felt the rejection, and the other part of me knew Jesus would take care of me. I praise my Lord and Savior Jesus Christ! He heard my prayers and led me to some God-fearing people who loved me and helped me start a brand new life. Truly God blesses us with more than enough when we obey the Word of God. I learned the true meaning of walking together in unity with others and laying down one's life for a friend. *"Greater love hath no man than this, that a man lay down his life for his friends."* (John 15:13)

A light of revelation shone in my heart; the lies that I had been taught were exposed and the truth was established. What I had grown up with was the fear of man. It dawned in my spirit that I needed God-fearing people to teach me to walk in the fear of the Lord.

"Come, ye children, hearken unto me: I will teach you the fear of the LORD." (Psa. 34:11)

"The fear of the Lord is the beginning of wisdom..." (Prov. 9:10) The fear of the Lord makes us wise so we may learn to discern the truth of who God is and who we are in Him. To fear God is to stand in awe of His greatness because He is Holy, Almighty, All Powerful and Creator of everything. I fear God and my heart's desire is to live for Him. Jesus is my life! I was created for a specific purpose for His glory. He loves and cherishes me, and I am accepted by Him.

Without the fear of God I walked in the fear of man. God is the only one that is to be feared. I had no other purpose or hope than to look to people for acceptance and fulfillment. Under the Hutterite teaching, I was vulnerable, numb, and void of understanding. I was fooled into thinking that if I worked hard enough and tortured myself, I would be loved and accepted by those to whom I was enslaved. Now I am a bondservant for Jesus Christ.

[6] "Not with eyeservice, as menpleasers; but as the servants of Christ, doing the will of God from the heart;"

[7] "With good will doing service, as to the Lord, and not to men:" (Eph. 6:6-7)

Salvation is not of works, it is by grace through faith. Works alone don't prove our love for Jesus. Jesus sacrificed Himself once, for all people. I now enjoy my life in Jesus because of my relationship with Him. To follow Jesus Christ is to have Him as one's first love. A Christian is one who knows Jesus Christ personally and intimately. Jesus is more than just a storybook character that you read about. It takes open, transparent communication to get to know someone. It's the same when getting to know Jesus Christ. By learning to hear the Lord's voice one can get to know Him. I wholeheartedly choose to be obedient when the Lord speaks to me. It is a joy unspeakable to hear His voice, walk in the Spirit, and glorify God, the Holy One of Israel.

Only after leaving the colony did I discover I was anorexic. My addiction to starving was brought to a close when the Lord revealed that the oppression of man-made principles plunges a man's soul into darkness. I received help and full deliverance through the blood of Jesus Christ and discipleship, where I realized my worth to God and His unconditional love for me. Praise the Lord, now that the Holy Spirit breathes life into me I am no longer just rattling bones. My husband remarks he can hardly imagine I'm the same person I was when we met six years ago. He saw that I was not only physically undernourished, but also spiritually starving. He's always encouraging me to find my confidence in Jesus Christ and step out of the past comfort zones in which I was set. I could operate with joy and peace when I began overcoming my fears. Once I came to my right mind, the torment subsided and I could eat without condemnation. It took prevailing prayer and God surrounding me with people who loved me enough to tell me the truth. That gave me the victory to confidently say:

[2] "Bless the LORD, O my soul, and forget not all his benefits:"

[3] "Who forgiveth all thine iniquities; who healeth all thy diseases;"

[4] "Who redeemeth thy life from destruction; who crowneth thee with lovingkindness and tender mercies;"

[5] "Who satisfieth thy mouth with good things; so that thy youth is renewed like the eagle's." (Psa. 103:2-5)

I boast in the Lord for all the awesome things He has done for me.

Now, I can praise the Lord with lifted hands, dancing feet, and singing lips, knowing I am loosed from those demonic patterns of thinking.

CHAPTER 9

Oh, That Valley Of Decision

Joel 3:14 "Multitudes, multitudes in the valley of decision: for the day of the LORD is near in the valley of decision."

Junia Waldner:
Junia was born in Manitoba, Canada and is now a citizen of the United States. She is gifted with a green thumb and has a passion for all types of gardening. Summer is her favorite season as she loves being outdoors and delights in watching trees, flowers, and vegetables grow to maturity. Her smile is contagious and she brings happiness to those around her. Junia's calling in obedience to God leads her to pray and wait upon the Lord at the Throne of Grace. She is patient, spiritually sensitive, and accurate in delivering God's Word to the weary and those who need encouragement. Junia diligently works with her sister Cindy in a cleaning business. Attending several symphonies and listening to the brass instruments inspired her to learn to play the trumpet to the glory of God.

I am writing my testimony in the fear of Almighty God. My prayer is that it would be beneficial to anyone who will read it. God has worked in my heart to bring me to a place of whole-hearted dependence on and dedication to Jesus Christ. I am delighted to share the freedom I have found in my Lord and Savior Jesus Christ.

I grew up as a Hutterite. My prescribed task was the same as any other Hutterite woman: get married and have children. I was very unhappy. Once I came to the age of responsibility, my dream was to be drawn out of the shell that kept me without joy, alone, and without any friends. I dreamed of being outgoing and joyful. I wanted to know the purpose for my life and go for it, not follow what everyone else was doing – like sheep led to the slaughter. An assignment was imposed upon me leading me on a downward path, an overshadowing that smothered my dreams. I learned to become a silent, skittish, and self-conscious person borne out of fear and shame that had affected my life ever since I was a young Hutterite girl. For those who might think the Hutterite life is a wholesome, protected, loving, and innocent place for kids, let me tear away the curtain and reveal the way it really is.

As a girl, many restraints were placed on me involving commonplace activities that many children enjoy. I loved being outside and riding a bike in summertime with my friends. It would have been so much more fun if we didn't have to scurry for the bushes to hide our bikes, or crouch in the ditches every time we saw the minister or German schoolteacher coming. Girls weren't permitted to ride bikes or ice skate. In the dark of night some of us would sneak down to the pond to ice skate. We were scared and constantly looking over our shoulders, but eager to escape our dull daily routine. Boys were allowed to skate and bike freely, why not us? This angered me because we were never given a reason. I wasn't asking for much! I remember standing with the other young girls at the minister's doorstep, begging and pleading for permission to go to the nearby winter fair like the boys did every year. He adamantly refused and coldly turned us away. I felt belittled, worthless, and rejected because I was a girl.

After the minister had his own granddaughter, who wanted to ride bikes and skate, he loosened the reins on some of these restrictions. With tumultuous waves of unreasonable, weighty burdens absent of God's love, there can be no true discipline that yields the peaceable fruit of righteousness. Man-made rules and customs will produce rebellion, which eventually causes a heart to be hardened against the truth and insensitive to the promptings of the human conscience. This is the result of a lack of loving, personal care for the eternal state of the souls of people. The double standard and unfair lifestyle cultivated rebellion in my heart to the place where the consequences wouldn't completely stop me from doing what I wanted to do. I just did it more sneakily to avoid getting caught.

In its present condition, the Hutterite religion does not operate according to the Word of God and thus, cannot glorify God. The Hutterites have their own interpretation of scriptures brought about by man's soulish reasoning and not the revelation borne of the Holy Spirit, which produces freedom and life.

My brother was excommunicated because he stood for the truth in the Word of God instead of the traditions of the Hutterite church. My dad stood in agreement with my brother and my parents ended up losing their position as colony members. In July of 2006 our family attended my other brother's wedding outside the colony. The very next day the leaders used the fabricated excuse of the wedding to excommunicate my two sisters and me. The real reason for our excommunication was that we had accepted Jesus Christ as our Lord and Savior. I was commanded not to work, or go to church, or be involved in any colony activities. I knew then, I would have to leave the colony. I was very confused. I did not know what to do or where I would go. I never imagined that something like this could ever happen to me. My own uncle, the colony minister, initiated and executed the excommunication. I was ill prepared for any other life than the one where every move and decision are dictated.

139

In the months following I heard about a ministry in the United States through stirring reports from Hutterites and ex-Hutterites who had visited this ministry. This was most welcome news after long months of hopeless frustration. Soon after, some of the members of my family and I visited that ministry. I was refreshed by the Holy Spirit and built up by the Word of God that was shared that day. After much prayer we were cordially invited by the leadership to come for discipleship. I prayed and immediately knew I would get the restoration I needed, coming out of a situation of control and bondage that affected me spiritually, mentally, and physically.

At the time of leaving the colony, I discovered that only through Jesus Christ could I be set free and become all He wants me to be. In order to receive full deliverance and healing, there was something I needed to do. I needed to give up selfishness and pride, which go against truly being dependent upon and trusting in the Lord. At the ministry I was taught what the Word of God says on how to live as a Christian woman. The Lord Jesus started to bring a change in my life. I finally saw a vision of a truly fulfilling life. Yet, I had to seriously ask myself, "Am I really willing to pay the price?"

"Then said Jesus unto His disciples, if any man will come after me, let him deny himself, and take up his cross, and follow me." (Matt. 16:24)

If anyone desires to follow Him, he must count the cost of being a disciple of Jesus Christ.

I wanted to follow Jesus Christ and reap the fruit of discipleship without the uncomfortable pruning and tilling that goes along with it. I wanted the benefits without the work and accountability. Anyone who truly walks with the Lord Jesus knows that cannot work. After almost five years of discipleship in a Christian ministry, receiving teaching and training according to the Word of God, my heart was divided because I was still strong willed and stubborn. That's right, a stubborn and rebellious believer who selfishly wanted her own way.

Yes, God did bring change in my life in those five years, but it was only as much as I allowed Him to. I missed out by not being submitted to Jesus one hundred percent. The people God blessed me with loved me so much they would not allow me to continue half-heartedly. They knew God's heart for me and saw my potential in Christ Jesus. Would I follow Jesus with all my heart and continue to be discipled, or leave and be swallowed up by the works of my own flesh? I was double-minded and I lacked the peace and joy because I wanted to somehow preserve those little areas of false security, which were actually killing me.

On October 20, 2011, I went to stay with my parents in Canada to hopefully work out issues in my heart, and allow God to bring me to a place of brokenness in the fear of the Lord and learn to be totally dependent upon Him. I needed to learn to not rely on people to make decisions for me, which is the easy way and always the worst way. I was influenced in the colony for 22 years by a religion that led me without Jesus being the sole motivation, causing spiritual laziness and complacency in my life. I was in torment, a result of not trusting and relying on Jesus, my Lord and Savior.

The time it takes to make the changes necessary to be fully willing and obedient to the Lord Jesus Christ depends on the person's heart condition and her desperation. While at my parent's house God put me through a test to prove whether I would stand and become stronger or go back to my crippling, familiar ways. Those who were professing Christianity were speaking against the elementary principles of the Word of God. They lacked the biblical understanding by the revelation of the Holy Spirit. Therefore, I was in a state of confusion because I put myself there. I was stubbornly fighting against the Lord by staying there. They weren't confident they could hear from the Lord, therefore I couldn't receive what they were saying as truth. I knew in my heart I didn't fit in there and I never would.

I praise God for what I learned in those five years in the U.S. and the foundation that was laid, so I could be confident in what I knew to be true according to the Word of God.

I stayed at my parents' home in Manitoba for about a month, and the Lord called me to go visit my brother who lives in an excommunicated Hutterite Christian Community in Saskatchewan. I'm blessed to say I met some precious people while I was there and I love them. It broke my heart to see people in this Christian Community who desired to walk in unity and oneness with the Lord, yet lacked the wisdom and understanding of the pattern that Jesus ordered as His example of discipleship led by the Holy Spirit. Leaders must lovingly care for the hearts of the people to teach and train them, showing them the way to freedom and how to experience righteousness, peace, and joy in the power of the Holy Spirit.

I am thankful to the Lord for the discipleship I received, and the godly leadership that taught me how to hear the voice of God. One cannot enter into the intimate relationship the Lord desires to have with His children without hearing the voice of God. This is why many Christians never come to full maturity and to the revelation and understanding of who they are in Jesus Christ. How can a leader tend the flock of God without hearing the Lord's voice, knowing God's heart for each individual in his care? Scripture says in Prov. 27:23: *"Be thou diligent to know the state of thy flocks, and look well to thy herds."*

While I was away from the ministry in the United States, I listened to what ex-Hutterites around me in Canada were saying against what I know is true, and I began to question. Was God leading me in a totally different direction than what I thought was right? Was it possible that the ministry where I had been was actually not where God wanted me to be any longer?

Through many nights and days of desperately seeking God's will for my life it was still not clear to me where God was leading me. When the time at my brother's place came to an end, I returned to my parents' home in Manitoba. After only a few spiritually uneventful days of going nowhere at my parents' home, I decided to go to another ex-Hutterite's home I had only visited once before. The husband there was respected by my parents as being spiritually mature. I went there believing he and his wife would be able to offer me spiritual counsel for my situation. But if I had considered their counsel I would have had to leave behind the most basic, fundamental truths I knew in my heart to be true. After hearing many hours of their opinions it was obvious they could not offer me any solid godly counsel or leadership, and certainly no clear direction for my life.

By now I was weary, and I needed revelation of the Holy Spirit to bring comfort and peace to my heart.

I was seriously considering my two options:

Option #1: Walk away from the ministry where I had been trained and forget the calling God has on my life. I would find a church where I could be comfortable with little accountability. Then find a guy, get married, and have children.

Option #2: Return to the ministry in the United States; follow Jesus with all my heart, love Him and walk in His righteousness and justice. In this ministry I would continue to be raised up in the calling that God had ordained for me from the foundation of the world. I would grow in and exercise the gifts God has given me.

And I admit, because of my headstrong stubbornness and spiritual laziness I chose option #1. On January 17th I went to get all my belongings to leave the ministry in the U.S. for good. I was feeling numb inside. I was not fully settled with the choice I had just made but was going ahead with it anyway. Can you imagine a saved, born again Christian walking in such bold-faced rebellion?

I gathered my belongings, talked to a few of the people there and walked out. Wow! What mixed feelings! I had just separated from the ministry, the place that was home, and the people who were family to me for the past five years. I felt sad, but strangely in my heart I felt no separation from them. What I felt was a deeper love for all of them and knew without a doubt they cared for my spiritual well-being. Some of the people I had visited or associated with outside this little ministry would show concern for how I was doing physically and emotionally rather than spiritually in Christ Jesus. They could not offer me any more than what they understood or knew because of their lack of true discipleship in Jesus Christ. In the days after I left the ministry, people often asked me how I was doing. I would tell them I was doing very well. They could not know it was due to the love and prayers I continued to receive from the ministry in the U.S.

After leaving the ministry in the United States I saw how blessed I was to have been discipled by godly leadership which was for my safety and protection. By physically walking away, the Lord caused me to realize what I had really left behind. I knew my heart was with that ministry and that's where He wanted me to be.

Five years previous to this, when I chose to be part of the ministry in the U.S., I was just going along with all the others, hanging onto their coattails. This time, January 26, 2012, I chose option #2 with my whole-hearted conviction to follow Jesus and be a disciple of Him! Immediately the fullness of freedom and joy flooded my heart, the backward child faded away, and the bold, outgoing woman I always desired to be finally rose out of the ashes.

Most of the people and family members I visited in Canada had one thing in common. They all claim to have left the Hutterite system to serve and follow the Lord Jesus Christ. Unfortunately, everyone I met who had come out of the Hutterite system was without godly leadership and true discipleship. Fear and the lack of knowledge of the Word of God caused them to judge with harsh suspicion and reject any leadership, even those ordained by God. As Hutterites they had grown up under a false authority, which ultimately ruled over them for the colony's selfish gain. My spirit was grieved when the scripture Matthew 9:36 was quickened to me: *"But when he saw the multitudes, he was moved with compassion on them, because they fainted, and were scattered abroad, as sheep having no shepherd."*

Jesus Christ took me out of the Hutterite system physically, and through His grace and power He has also delivered my soul from the bondage and fear I lived in as a Hutterite. I have made a free will commitment to follow Jesus Christ and watch His heart's desire come to pass in my life. It is a blessing to see my dreams come true and experience how God is using me in the purposes for which I was put on this earth.

I am now fulfilling my calling as an intercessor in prayer. I pray to know God's heart in matters and hear His voice, and walk in obedience in what He wants me to do, where He wants me to go, and when He wants me to do it.

I love to minister to people by serving them and sharing with them my experiences of the unconditional love of God. I visit people in hospitals, assisted living, and private homes, and pray for them. For those who are willing I pray with them to receive salvation through Jesus Christ.

When I was a Hutterite woman, I did not have the freedom to minister to people outside of the colony. I could not have a driver's license and did not think I was capable of driving a car because it always seemed so difficult. Now that I have my driver's license I really love to drive. I have driven a pickup truck with a trailer and have had the opportunity to operate a skid-steer loader on a farm. I've flown in a commercial airliner and have had some flying lessons in a private airplane. Some of what is considered "man's work" in the colony, I now love to do. I've learned to use a chainsaw safely when cutting trees and I help my brothers in the Lord with roofing jobs in their construction business. I was not created to just cook, clean, and garden, even though I love doing it. I have my own cleaning business and work together with my sisters. I earn my own money and spend it where the Lord leads me, and I buy the style of clothes I want to wear. I am no longer restricted to wearing a Hutterite dress and head covering. Imagine, I used to have to wear this cumbersome outfit at all times, even when exercising, jogging, or participating in water activities. God looks at the heart, and what matters most to God is that we love Him and prove it by loving other people. A simple, God-fearing life is freeing!

There is always something that can motivate a person's heart. Gardening has always been one of the things that stirs my heart. When I put that little seed from my hand into the ground and water it, I realize the miracle God does every time one of those little seeds grows. I remember when I was just a little girl I would spend hours playing in the dirt and planting my own garden of weeds. If you had asked me I would have told you I had the most beautiful weed garden in the whole world. As an adult in the colony I was required to work in the garden, where one could expect an argument to break out at any moment. I was constantly on edge and quickly lost the desire for and joy of gardening because of the friction and disunity. The very thing I loved to do was no longer enjoyable.

After I left the colony, I was blessed to be in charge of a very large garden. I could choose what to plant, where to plant it, and how much of it to plant. This was a welcome responsibility I never had as a Hutterite woman. It was a bit frightening at first, but I soon realized how much I still loved gardening. It is a blessing to have the freedom to share produce with people in need, who appreciate and enjoy it.

I take great pleasure in making desserts for people, cooking a meal to take to people's homes, or inviting friends over for a dinner party. There are many, many things I enjoy doing that were never possible in a Hutterite colony.

During the summer months I spend a lot of time at a lake swimming, camping, and waterskiing. At times when I just want to relax and have a good time, I enjoy going fishing. When doing those things with Jesus ever present, it is so peaceful and seems like nothing else in the world matters.

Learning to swim is very important to me after I had a near drowning experience. I encourage every person to learn to swim, not only for yourself but because someday you might have to save someone who can't swim, or is injured and in serious trouble. I often wonder if I could overcome the guilt of being responsible for someone drowning, knowing I could have saved him had I been able to swim. What would have happened if someone had not been there for me when I was drowning? So, I heeded the wisdom of Jesus Christ and took swimming lessons. Praise God I can now swim and be safe.

As it is my responsibility to learn how to swim so I can save others, so it is also my responsibility as a Christian to preach the Word of God to people without hope, and see them come to salvation through faith in Jesus Christ.

"And others save with fear, pulling them out of the fire; hating even the garment spotted by the flesh." (Jude 1:23)

"...how shall they hear without a preacher?" (Rom. 10:14)

Constant loneliness and fear, shame and depression once defined my life. I now walk in the light and have victory over the strongholds of darkness through my Lord and Savior Jesus Christ.

CHAPTER 10

The Hutterite Golden Boy

Jason Waldner:
At age 22 Jason left a Hutterite colony in North Dakota. His dad is a well-known Hutterite German schoolteacher. Jason was religiously dedicated to the Hutterite rules and culture. He was driven by the obsessive aspiration of having the most powerful position of monetary control in the colony. The colony secretary position would satisfy his lust for power and stature. An unhealthy competition and stubborn drive was ingrained in him through the Hutterite system. Unknown to Jason and despite his most "lofty goal," God had ordained for him a much higher calling. Through circumstances God began opening Jason's eyes to see how the system was corrupt and failing. Disillusioned, Jason left the colony in October 2006 for a place where he learned how to follow Jesus, and God brought deliverance from the religious oppression and legalism through discipleship. Jason is now married to the love of his life, Karen. He is a partner in a successful construction company and excels in computer design. He enjoys physical activities such as waterskiing and snow skiing.

The air felt more stuffy than usual in the church basement. Everything was deathly quiet except for the preacher reading the list of rules made and announced annually by the Hutterite leaders. I was to obey these legalistic rules in order to be considered a good Hutterite. I couldn't help but wonder if my peers were noticing my inner turmoil as I sat shoulder to shoulder, surrounded by a sea of religious people dressed in black.

I knew in my heart what I had to do: Stand up and walk out. I knew it was right to walk out and to show my disagreement with what was being read. But even more than opposition, I felt disdain for the hypocrisy and errors I was hearing. Yet I was thinking, "Walk out? What would everyone else think?" In this state of hesitation I began to feel a mixture of anger and fear. I had never done anything like this!

I grew up believing that if I obeyed the rules set forth by the Hutterite Church it would serve as my ticket to heaven. This was one of those times when I realized the traditions of the Hutterite elders were contrary to the written Word of God. There were such ordinances as forbidding fellowship with a colony that was excommunicated from the Hutterite Church for their faith in Jesus Christ. The new rules also prohibited any Hutterite colony from having a Christian curriculum in their English school.

I began to see all of this as it really is and a righteous anger rose up within me as I realized I conformed to believe these lies. I was asking myself, "Am I the only one feeling this frustration… Why isn't someone standing up for the truth?" Deception was blinding the very people who were supposed to lead me spiritually. Was it ever going to change? Could I ever learn to follow and walk day to day with Jesus Christ in such an environment?

The Holy Spirit was revealing Himself by His convicting power. I grew up trying to obey the teachings of the Hutterite Church and would always be the one to stand up for the Hutterite way of life. My dad was a well-known, respected religious teacher. I was diligent at my work, respected by the leaders as I obeyed and performed to their high expectations. I was a golden boy. With my mind racing, I stayed frozen in the pew. The air felt even stuffier than before. My heart was stirred and convicted as the Spirit of truth was pounding at the very core of my being. What I now wholeheartedly know as truth is in direct violent opposition to the way I was raised and taught to believe as a Hutterite: that the Hutterite doctrine and way of life were the only way to please God. Well, if not the only way, then, of course, far superior to anything else, so I thought.

At that moment I didn't know the decision I was about to make would impact other lives as well. But I recognized I was miserable, empty, and I desperately needed Jesus Christ in all of my life.

My heart cried out with deepened conviction: I can't stay here! Not in this hypocrisy! Not without love!

I began to grasp that the type of love I was receiving, or had received growing up, was not the unconditional love borne by the Holy Spirit. I believed my parents loved me. Why didn't they stand up against the system that had shown such favoritism towards some, and left others to scrounge for themselves? In so many ways this system's operation is much more slanted towards prejudice and selfish competition than the outside world.

Our family was very low in the power structure in the colony where I grew up in the United States. The discrepancies in how some members were treated versus others might not seem huge to you, yet the impact sure felt huge as a child. And lest I forget the discrimination, there were daily examples to remind me of how low I was in that well patterned scheme of a power structure. It was very successful in depleting life and morale. I was empty and dry, merely going through the motions to please those in authority over me.

Why the inequality? One main reason was nepotism. Nepotism is favoritism based on kinship.

I was raised in an ongoing power struggle between two main families while the rest were caught in the middle. The power struggle permeated into the classroom where my dad taught the German language and the Hutterite religion. This struggle even reached the children's dining room where my parents oversaw the children. When I was about 10 years old I witnessed a child's father storm into the children's dining room. He began yelling at my mom in front of us about a disagreement he had with my dad about disciplining his child. Witnessing these common outbursts of anger, and never seeing bridges of sincere reconciliation built, caused the children to fall into the same pattern. With this continued tension between the parents, I would choose to play or hang out with some and not with others and certainly would not visit their homes.

As a child I also experienced inequality with recreational items such as bicycles, rollerblades, and hockey equipment. I could never understand why some "had" and others "had not." Everything was supposed to be shared, common, and equal. I was tormented by the anger rising within. What was happening to me was wrong! I knew it! The money to buy such items wasn't given by the colony. I would secretly collect some scrap copper or pop cans and recycle them for money. These opportunities to make money were scarce because it was prohibited to make any money for one's own use. Everything from my time to the clothes on my back belonged to the colony. By forbidding the making of money for one's own use, the colony had almost complete control over my whole life. Others in the colony had things I could never have and it was very frustrating and degrading.

I didn't have the money, and had only rare opportunities to pocket any. Were others stealing money? Is this why they had more than me? My parents worked just as hard as anyone else in the colony, yet they couldn't buy us the things other children had. It was nearly impossible for my parents to get any money, even for very basic items around the house. Intimidated by the leaders, feeling helpless, I kept quiet.

The communal lifestyle of "equality" I experienced as a Hutterite was a constant struggle for a share of the pie and a vying for a desirable position on the social ladder within the colony. The Hutterite elders will tell you that everything in the colony belongs to everyone. However, I have lived under this system and I tell you the truth, within this system there are the "haves" and the "have nots."

The Hutterites' communal living is often compared to communism. Both Hutterism and communism can't live up to a mainstay of "equality." The concept of communism, even socialism, may sound wonderful to most people. Don't be fooled. The more one allows others to feed and take care of one instead of relying on God, the fewer rights, freedoms, and privileges one has under such tyrants.

The saying "absolute power corrupts absolutely" is so true. Hutterite leaders boast in saying they take care of an individual from the cradle to the grave. But, at what a price! For someone to lose one's personal identity, to lose freedom and liberty, and maybe even one's soul for a false hope, is beyond what I can express.

My parents had to deal with the unfair practices and favoritism when asking the leaders for permission to take our family to visit relatives at other Hutterite colonies. Everybody was out for himself and watched others with a selfish jealousy. Partiality and preferential treatment were commonplace. As I became older, the nepotism reared its ugly head in other ways. I always enjoyed math and had dreams of learning how to be an architectural engineer. I loved to work with computers and wanted to learn how to write software. I also had a desire to learn carpentry, electric wiring, or welding. I wanted to work with my hands in something that would give me a sense of worth. Desperately I cried inside for this because I felt worthless. I had yet to experience who I was in Jesus Christ and know the love of God and the plans He had for me, the plans of freedom and joy. This I could not have learned or known within that closed-society lifestyle.

The Hutterites in their closed society are much the same as the caste system in India. A caste system is a division of society based on differences of wealth, inherited rank or privilege, profession, occupation, or race. In a caste system, to leave the "class" into which one is born is virtually impossible. Theoretically, in the Hutterite's communal lifestyle there is supposed to be equal opportunity. Yet, quite the opposite is true for those who happen to be born into a family that isn't well liked by the leaders. Like the caste system of India, it is difficult to progress within the colony's hierarchy.

So where did I end up working? A huge chicken barn! Ninety thousand chickens is an overwhelming responsibility for a young man. No one asked me, or considered what I wanted to do; the job was just assigned. Jobs are appointed by the leaders or voted on by the adult male members. I would have loved to counsel with my dad, discussing options and deciding a career path, as would be common in most families outside the colony.

I saw many jobs given to people because of favored family lines with little or no consideration for the individual's aptitude, skills, desires, or wishes. After all, how would leaders within the colony know the person's wishes? The leaders showed very little interest in me as an individual. There was no care as to who I was or what I wanted in life, unless, of course, it fit their agenda of slave labor.

Nepotism touched every area of life within the colony. When I went to ask the secretary for business-related money to do colony work, he always gave it reluctantly. It was humiliating and I felt like a beggar scrounging for scraps. Why did I have to beg for money to eat so I could continue working for the colony? I must have been born on the wrong side of the tracks. I felt guilty asking for money that was just as much mine as his. Why? At times, I would rather not ask for money and just not eat while on the egg delivery route which was regularly five days a week, often in excess of 100 miles from the colony to deliver the eggs. It usually took all day to make my rounds to the grocery stores. I would eat as cheaply as I could to save one or two dollars, in order to stretch the little I was given as far as possible. Isn't this very interesting when the colony grosses millions of dollars annually? I was an immature and naïve 16 year old when I started hauling eggs with a large straight truck and I didn't know how to drive it safely. It was during potato harvest, the busiest time of the year; I was suddenly given a mountain of responsibility with inadequate training, which led to error and dangerous situations. There were no safety instructions or standards set by those in charge over me when it came to working around machines, dust in the chicken barn, manure, etc. I found myself having to haul all the eggs, take care of all the chickens, and fix the chicken barn machines. I had no idea how they worked or how to fix them. In those times of frustration and anger I cried out to the Lord and I knew He heard my cry.

This unfair, degrading treatment defined a life I detested and it was shaping me into something I couldn't bear to become. So, as I sat frozen in that pew I chose what

I knew was right. For me, the Hutterite way of life and their way of church were over. But I was too scared to take a stand and walk out by myself. I walked out of church with everyone else as usual. That day I made the decision to leave which would prove to be the turning point in my life, even though overwhelming fear had kept me from publicly making a stand. There was now a glimmer of hope. What I experienced at that church service and the revelation God gave me concerning all this would not be in vain. Leaving the colony was now just a matter of time. Due to the social and moral imbalance in the treatment of the people and the numerous crystal-clear contradictions I witnessed, I had reached my limit. The continual sense of rejection I experienced growing up as a Hutterite was what finally brought my heart to say, "Enough!" And I meant it.

I walked home and made my resolve known to my peers. I needed a car in which to leave, just enough money, and a place to go. At that time I had nothing, but God's grace was abundantly sufficient. Beyond my meager resources God made a way while I struggled to put all the pieces together.

In the following days I would go on long walks and pray. I was crying out to the Lord, and God faithfully gave me clear direction to not partake of the Hutterite ceremony of communion. Receiving communion in the colony was an annual ceremony which took place in the spring of the year. This ceremony showed one's allegiance to the Hutterite faith. How could I take communion when I didn't agree with a single line of the elders' long list of written traditions, those very tenets that define a "good" Hutterite? My allegiance is to God and His Word. If the Hutterite ordinances are contrary to the Word of God then to what am I going to pledge my allegiance?

On the day of communion all the baptized members, dressed in black, entered the church with somber faces, sat for hours solemnly listening to a monotone reading, and finally partook of the bread and wine. This time I wasn't there. I had finally taken a stand. I didn't clearly know the consequences of not taking communion. Would I be excommunicated or punished in some other way? I had hope in God knowing I would soon be leaving this miserable life. This gave me joy and a clarity I'd never had before and I was getting excited. Months passed, and surprisingly the leaders never confronted me for not taking communion.

I diligently did my work at the chicken barn, but my heart wasn't in it. Summer was slowly fading away with harvest time approaching. I spent my spare time praying and reading the Bible. Stirred, yet waiting for whatever door would open so I could leave the colony. One day one of my brothers came home and told me about someone he had met who worked in one of the grocery stores where we delivered eggs for the colony. Can you imagine, someone who loved Jesus Christ and was part of a ministry that disciples people according to the Word of God? And even more, my brother was going to sneak away and visit that ministry very soon.

When my brother came back from his visit it was with excitement. Everything my brother told me about how the ministry operated was according to scripture. Well, of course I had to go and find out for myself. From the first visit, all the basic questions that the Hutterite faith could never answer were made plain, and everything was always based upon the Word of God.

A month after my first visit to the ministry, God miraculously provided a used car for me. A week before I left the colony I hid my new car in a garage in a town nearby. When the day came to leave the nervous anticipation was boiling over. I got up early and one of my brothers secretly took a colony vehicle to give me a ride to my car so I could leave. The feeling when I left the colony was heavenly and I was never going back ... ever!

Being discipled according to God's Word was a whole new world being opened unto me. Every day was filled with new experiences. I was surrounded by people who loved me and my heart was filled with thankfulness for God's amazing blessings. Accepting this godly love and patience wasn't easy after being in a performance mode of pleasing people for so long. Someone loving me unconditionally with no strings attached was hard for me to grasp. I was experiencing more freedom every day and knew in my heart the change was real. I could finally take a breath and enjoy everything God was doing around me.

The Holy Spirit was speaking, strongly impressing His burden upon my heart. Until now, my leaving had been largely about finding freedom for myself. God wanted more from me. I left on Oct. 11 and that very day He gave me a Bible verse: *"And the LORD said unto me, Arise, take thy journey before the people, that they may go in and possess the land, which I sware unto their fathers to give unto them."* (Deut. 10:11)

The Bible reference was the same number as the date I left, very fitting and easy to remember. God spoke to me that my deliverance was for the purpose of now helping others. God was faithfully drawing others out of the colony to experience the freedom found only in Jesus Christ. God wasn't allowing me to waste any time. We who had left the Hutterites were making phone calls, writing letters, and getting in touch with people within the Hutterite church: my parents, Hutterite leaders, and anyone who would desire the truth of the gospel of Jesus Christ. Searching souls were coming out of the Hutterite church and were following the Lord Jesus Christ into a life of victory.

There was opposition, especially from my family in the colony. I tried my best to be patient and to explain the new life I was now living. My family could not understand the changes Jesus Christ had brought into my life. The ever-widening gap in our strained relationship manifested when I wanted to attend my brother's wedding back in the colony. I showed up several hours before the wedding reception and I got a sick feeling in my stomach when I saw the look on my dad's face; he did not want his own son to be there when it was to be a joyous time of family celebration. My parents told me if I went to the wedding reception I would be kicked out. I simply got up and left.

"...For why is my liberty judged of another man's conscience?" (1 Cor. 10:29)

Paul was judged by legalistic people who didn't understand the change in his life. When Jesus Christ sets us free it is to serve Him in liberty, not to go back to religious bondage.

[35] "For I am come to set a man at variance against his father, and the daughter against her mother, and the daughter in law against her mother in law."

[36] "And a man's foes shall be they of his own household."

[37] "He that loveth father or mother more than me is not worthy of me: and he that loveth son or daughter more than me is not worthy of me." (Matt. 10:35-37)

Are we not obligated to help our fellow man when we see him being victimized? Every U.S. citizen has a God-given moral obligation to stand against oppression, whether emotional, physical, spiritual, or financial. Those who are established in truth and justice must judge, speak, and act in boldness against such forms of malicious control. The web of deceit that had entrapped us for so many years had to be exposed. The abuses had to stop. Like Moses when he went to speak to Pharaoh in Exodus 8:1: *"And the LORD spake unto Moses, Go unto Pharaoh, and say unto him, Thus saith the LORD, Let my people go, that they may serve me."*

Hutterite ministers are afraid the abuses and lies will be brought to light. With over 400 colonies, worth tens of millions each, there are billions of dollars at stake. They boast that all the colony's wealth is for their widows, orphans, and the sick. My experience was the opposite. Something that continues to disturb me is the lack of love towards people that are mentally challenged. I once read that God puts people less fortunate than ourselves in our path to see how we will respond to them. Do we have compassion, love and respect for these precious souls, or take advantage of them? Neither children nor adults respected the mentally challenged. One instance I witnessed left a young man sprawling in a pile of packaging boxes after a confrontation with two adults. In another instance I saw a woman falling off a wagon after being intentionally, "playfully" pushed. To this very day I can still vividly recall seeing the hurt faces and the tears.

If one hasn't been loved, one won't know how to love others. True love is rarely found within the performance-based Hutterite society. If you worked hard, you were more likely to be accepted. Of course, you also have to be born as a Hutterite and most preferably be white. Racial prejudice is alive and kicking in this "commune of love." Yes, by now this shouldn't surprise you.

One thing was clear to us as Hutterites: We were far loftier than the rest of the world. After all, we had the corner on going to heaven and these pompous dictates weren't just limited to our religion. It diabolically spilled over into a "Super-race" mentality, leading to prejudice against Blacks,

Native Americans, Asians, etc. Much of the prejudice was ingrained in me from a very young age.

I remember my dad telling me about a person of Japanese heritage who desired to join a particular Hutterite colony, but was rejected partly because of his heritage. My Dad told the story so I believe it to be true. I was warned many times that marriages between blacks and whites would not work out and should not ever happen. The Word of God states in Numbers 12 that Moses married Zipporah, a black woman. When Moses' sister Miriam criticized their marriage because of Zipporah's heritage, Miriam was cursed with leprosy. She was healed only by the grace of God after she truly repented. Why was this biblical account never brought to the forefront to teach the Hutterite children about racial prejudice?

While I was still in the colony, four people came from the outside to minister the gospel of Jesus Christ. One of them was a black man. When he talked with me afterwards, he shared the disdain he felt from the Hutterites and the looks he received when he was sitting with the Hutterite men (leadership was present), eating in the communal dining hall. He remarked that it felt as though he was visiting the "super-race." This was a young man, married, with two young children. He was polite and was dressed respectably.

What I am about to write is fundamentally important. I speak for myself and others who are writing their testimonies in these chapters. We have been rejected and scorned for telling the truth. We are testifying according to scriptural truth in the Word of God and our hearts are most certainly without malice, jealousy, greed, or unforgiveness.

While in the ministry where I was being discipled, we ex-Hutterites attempted to keep open doors of communication with the Hutterites. We contacted some of the elders on the committee that oversaw the colonies we left. They refused to meet with us. Did the leaders desire to maintain a status quo? Perhaps they see themselves at the top of the food chain. If it's worked so far, why change?

We made repeated efforts to bring hope in those areas of conflict and end the abuses. We desired to lovingly secure a resolution according to the Word of God with the Hutterite peoples. The only avenue and recourse left was to submit to the God-ordained authority as it says in Romans 13:1-5. We appealed to the justice system of North Dakota and started a lawsuit against our home colony. We did this to help the downtrodden, with a heart of compassion and not out of revenge. In a courtroom the injustices and illegal activities could finally be exposed and brought to light.

The web of deceit the Hutterites had woven will eventually be torn apart. For too long all this has been hidden behind a veil of secrecy, using religion as a cloak of covetousness, as it says in scripture (1 Thess. 2:5). Hutterite elders have perverted the constitutional right of the freedom of religion to exploit the colony members' right to worship God according to their conscience. When the final judgment of God is ruled, all unrighteousness will be exposed and those who have exercised ungodly rule over men will be justly charged for every act. My prayer for those who are guilty is that God will touch their hearts and they would repent of those issues before that great and dreadful day.

[4] "For I know nothing by myself; yet am I not hereby justified: but he that judgeth me is the Lord."

[5] "Therefore judge nothing before the time, until the Lord come, who both will bring to light the hidden things of darkness, and will make manifest the counsels of hearts: and then shall every man have praise of God." (1 Cor. 4:4-5)

I couldn't serve Jesus Christ according to the standard of the Word of God in the colony. I had seen and heard numerous examples of people being disciplined and even excommunicated from the Hutterite church for believing basic biblical truths.

When I left the colony the Hutterites gave me nothing, even though I had spent years working for them. They were enriching themselves at the expense of the people who were kept ignorant of the God-given freedoms we have as citizens of the United States. The Hutterite leadership had hoodwinked me into signing different legal documents. It always seemed to be at hurried, inopportune times when I was rushing to work or at meal times, and the secretary's daughter was hasty and impatient to have the papers signed. They didn't allow me the time to read what I was signing. When I did ask they avoided telling me. This suspicious behavior later moved me to question if there were undisclosed documents and accounting records. Shadowy inner workings and lack of biblical transparency proves that God is not involved and is not being glorified.

I researched certain methods used in the colony's operations and discovered government documents that proved my name was used without my knowledge. I was actually named on those documents as a recipient of money from the United States Department of Agriculture to be used for purposes of generating income for the colony's interests. As a Hutterite I never saw the money or any documents. Those documents "proved" I was a percentage owner or investor of the colony. Why was nothing given to me when I asked the Hutterite leaders for restitution for all the years I worked for them?

How are the Hutterites able to claim government money for their business enterprises within the colony and not abide by the laws of the government? Somehow they don't have to abide by the same laws as any other business employer. For example, the labor laws in North Dakota are clearly defined concerning employees being recompensed for their time and effort. As a Hutterite, I wasn't made aware of any of my rights as an employee concerning minimum wage, overtime, and safety regulations, even child labor laws. The colony was filing tax returns on my behalf stating how much money I supposedly made for myself. All the money I "made" never touched my hands, never was saved for me, nor invested. It was always the colony's money.

I contacted the labor board of North Dakota, the United States Senators and Representative from North Dakota, drawing their attention to our plight. I personally handed the governor of North Dakota a packet concerning our desire for justice. They all responded positively to what we were doing, and most of them were willing to help if it was in their power to do so.

We went face-to-face with the Hutterites, sent letters, and made phone calls to hopefully resolve the issues outside the court of law. Going to court was a last option and if there was any possible way to reach a resolution without involving the courts, we would have gladly reconciled. When it came time for the judge to make a decision on whether to allow this case in a court of law, she dismissed the case stating, "The Court lacks subject matter jurisdiction to hear this case as it is a violation of the Establishment Clause of the First Amendment for this Court to intervene in questions regarding analysis and interpretation of church doctrine and ecclesiastical policy. The matter before this Court was already handled by the Board of Elders and the Conference Board of the Hutterite Church."

The legal counsel for the Hutterites purposely and grossly misrepresented the intent of our lawsuit, because it was never about religious disputes. Our focus was on the socio-economic abuses that were being inflicted upon the innocent. Our conscious decision to appeal to the courts was about ethics, principles, and common decency.

I wasn't moved when I heard the news about the judge's decision. I am rejoicing and in hot expectation of what God is going to do. I have seen injustices prevail for a season, but know this: at the end of the matter God always renders a righteous judgment and a true verdict. *"And Jesus looking upon them saith, with men it is impossible, but not with God: for with God all things are possible."* (Mark 10:27) This is just the beginning of the truth coming forth to expose the lies. We know it isn't over yet and we are not going to give up the battle. By the grace of God, I will continue to reach out to the Hutterites and all people with love and truth. Where I was raised and what I experienced helps me relate to people in similar situations. The problems within the Hutterite church aren't unique to just Hutterites. People who set up idolatrous kingdoms to hopefully deceive others for selfish gain must expect God's righteous judgment, and those kingdoms shall surely pass away.

My prayer is that people will come to the saving knowledge of Jesus Christ, learn to follow and serve Him, because He is the only way to God the Father and life everlasting.

What must I do to be saved?

In this world all humans are separated from God by sin.

"For <u>all have sinned</u>, and come short of the glory of God;" (Romans 3:23)

Confess and repent from your sins by leaving behind your old ways and be cleansed from all unrighteousness. Repentance requires a willingness to surrender to Jesus Christ, allowing Him to completely transform your life. It is impossible for man to attain salvation by his own works. It is possible only through faith in Jesus Christ.

"Jesus saith unto him, I am the way, the truth, and the life: no man cometh unto the Father, but by me." (John 14:6)

Father God sent His only begotten Son, Jesus Christ to earth, where He lived a perfect life free from all sin and died on the cross as a sacrifice for our sins.

"For God so loved the world, that he gave his only begotten Son, that whosoever believeth in him should not perish, but have everlasting life." (John 3:16)

On the third day He rose from the dead, triumphing over death and Satan. Jesus Christ is the only way man can receive forgiveness for his sins and be reconciled to God the Father.

"Neither is there salvation in any other: for there is none other name under heaven given among men, whereby we must be saved." (Acts 4:12)

You must first believe that Jesus Christ died for your sins and was raised from the dead on the third day. Then ask Jesus Christ into your heart to be the Lord and Savior of your life. When you confess with your mouth what you believe in your heart, He will come into your heart (your spirit) and you begin a new life in Him.

[9] "That if thou shalt confess with thy mouth the Lord Jesus, and shalt believe in thine heart that God hath raised him from the dead, thou shalt be saved."

[10] "For with the heart man believeth unto righteousness; and with the mouth confession is made unto salvation." (Romans 10:9-10)

To receive Jesus Christ as your Lord and Savior say this prayer:

Father God,

I come to you in the name of Jesus Christ, the only begotten Son of God.

I confess that I am a sinner and ask for forgiveness of my sins. I need you, Jesus.

Your Word says You are faithful and just to forgive my sins and cleanse me from all unrighteousness.

I believe and accept your love and mercy.

I repent and turn from my sins and I will follow you according to the Word of God.

I believe that Jesus Christ died on the cross for my sin. As your Word says, I confess with my mouth the Lord Jesus and believe in my heart that you, Father God, raised Jesus from the dead on the third day, and He is now seated at the right hand of the Father.

I receive you, Jesus Christ, into my heart as Savior and Lord of my life.

Thank you Father for your love and salvation and making me a new creation in Jesus Christ. I am now saved. I love you Jesus, and I will follow and serve you all the days of my life.

In Jesus' name, Amen

For spiritual growth in Jesus Christ, pray and allow the Lord to lead you into fellowship with likeminded believers. One needs to learn to walk as a disciple of Jesus Christ according to the Word of God.

When you receive Jesus Christ into your heart, the Word of God commands you to be baptized by full immersion in water. *"He that believeth and is baptized shall be saved..."* (Mark 16:16)

After you have received Jesus Christ and are baptized in water, God's desire is that you receive the promise of the fullness He has for every believer to walk in. Receive the baptism of the Holy Spirit.

[15] "Who, when they were come down, prayed for them, that they might receive the Holy Ghost:"

[16] "(For as yet he was fallen upon none of them: only they were baptized in the name of the Lord Jesus.)"

[17] "Then laid they their hands on them, and they received the Holy Ghost." (Acts 8:15-17)

And:

[38] "Then Peter said unto them, Repent, and be baptized every one of you in the name of Jesus Christ for the remission of sins, and ye shall receive the gift of the Holy Ghost."

[39] "For the promise is unto you, and to your children, and to all that are afar off, even as many as the Lord our God shall call." (Acts 2:38-39)